ABOUT THE AUTHOR

Catherine Bennett has worked for almost 30 years in a counselling capacity. She started her vocational work with the National Childbirth Trust in North West London and from then went on to study in Psychology formally. She trained in Person Centred Counselling, Psychodynamic Counselling and Cognitive Behavioural Therapy. She worked for a year at Strangeways Laboratory in Cambridge, for the chief Epidemiologist who worked on the relationship between DNA genetics and diet to find causal links with cancer.

Her Psychotherapy clinics have included a surgery in Cambridge, a private clinic in Haverhill and a Clinic (Cabinet) in Luxembourg.

Catherine has worked with children, adolescents and adults in a multi-disciplinary setting. She has worked with clients from all nationalities living in a multi-cultural setting in Luxembourg which she moved to in 1996. The problems that her clients have presented with are far ranging, but certainly for the purposes of this book she has referred to her experience of working with the bereaved in grief therapy.

After many years of therapeutic work Catherine decided to concentrate on her writing, which has always been a passion of hers. She is currently working on non-fiction pieces, fiction and comedy. In comedy she finds an outlet for truly authentic human emotions, stripped back and raw.

'ARE YOU AFRAID OF DEATH?'
'NO MORE THAN I WAS TO BE BORN'
'WHEN A FREE MAN DIES, HE LOSES THE PLEASURE OF
HIS LIFE. A SLAVE LOSES HIS PAIN. DEATH IS THE ONLY
FREEDOM A SLAVE KNOWS. THAT'S WHY HE'S NOT
AFRAID OF IT'

SPARTACUS

FOREWORD

Having worked as a Psychotherapist for most of my adult life, death and grieving has been an important component and content of my work. The stories that my clients have brought to me and trusted me with have affected me deeply and in their journey through grief, touched the very corner stone of what it means to be human and how the essence of death being present in our lives informs us. **Memento Mori** the Latin for **'remember you are mortal'.** We have it in our mind to help us live useful and productive lives, it helps us to not go AWOL. I have always been captivated by the notion of our purpose on earth, the drive to survive and how we deal with those we love who die. It is the most normal thing in the world to die. Just as normal as being born. And yet both those primitive actions are life changing in their physicality and affect. It is the moment when we connect most with our primitive self. We are not shielded from births now, in fact labour wards seemed rammed to the gills with onlookers, especially for the Kardashian family. No longer does the father smoke a cigar in a nearby waiting room until the midwife gives him the good news. No he's there at the action end, wondering if he will ever want to visit it again? But we still shield death in our culture. More so than in any other culture. The Catholics display open casket as do Baptists and Pentecostalists. Secular England hides and deals tastefully with death. The morgue to crematorium, more and more a choice with no congregation to witness the cremation. What becomes of us as humans if we change our rituals, if we ignore the physicality of death and let it lie in a shadow of professionals paid to deal with it?

Death is all around us. Inevitable. During 2019 the fear of an early death or a ghastly death has become a reality globally. The plague has hit us and made us face our mortality in a more immediate sense. We haven't just popped it on the back shelf to think about only when we are ill or when we decide we are getting old, or nearing the age where are parents/grandparents died.

What intrigues me is whether we deal better with death now than at other times or in other cultures? What is a good death? Do we mean a good death for the lost relative/friend or do we mean a good death for the griever?

Do we believe in the afterlife? Is there any evidence to suggest there is one? Are our individualistic ways of mourning helping us or hindering us?

There is a link between these questions and how we are increasingly attempting to be our own comforter in complex times. Never before has society become so ego driven. Not just in a narcissistic way, but in the sense that proposals, weddings and increasingly funerals have to be managed in individual expressions pertinent to the person involved and filmed for prosperity. Social media is now a norm for hearing about loss and expressing sentiments about the person online.

This book shall look at this evolving landscape and attempt to decipher what this means for our primitive drives, are we creating an anxiety ridden culture? Or have we got a handle on it?

INTRODUCTION

As mentioned, I have worked for many years with patients/clients who present with a great variety of problems. They may not appear in therapy with grief as their 'presenting issue', that is the issue that they have turned up to talk about and make sense of. But it is not uncommon for sessions to be stagnating until a death is mentioned and suddenly the emotions flow. This can cause embarrassment to the client who suddenly feels 'where did that come from?' It might be that the loss was 10 years ago and then as we talk through it we find that the grief has effectively been put on hold. That kids were born, house moves made, new jobs. Yes, they went to a funeral and cried. But there was no gap to mourn or process their grief. It can be that the grief has just lain around stopping the person from getting on with their life. They have become robotic and static. Suddenly accessing the grief can free the client from shut down emotions.

There is no 'one way fits all' for grieving. Not everyone can sit down sobbing for days as we seem to believe is the best thing for us. It comes when we allow it to in the form that is natural to us. We cannot diarize it seemingly.

We shall look at what it means to get stuck in grief. My mother got stuck in grief having given birth to a stillborn baby, the last baby she planned on having. The grief she felt immobilized her emotionally and, in my opinion, she never recovered from it. She could function as a teacher, with projects that she enjoyed, but she could no longer connect emotionally with us children or be the mother she had once been. She was violently against holding the dead baby. She was offered this, indeed encouraged to do this in Yeovil Maternity Hospital (1967) where she had to give birth in traditional fashion even though she had been told 3 weeks before that the baby was dead inside her. For some reason due to risk of hemorrhage the safest way was to have the baby induced on the natural due date. As children we had been told the baby was already dead, but aged 5, I thought they had maybe made a mistake and that the baby was hidden somewhere in the house. Of course denial is not just a river in Egypt. I realized at this very young age that death existed and it shaped my thinking and obsessive praying. I was terrified of something happening to my Mum or indeed to me. So I developed Obsessive Compulsive Disorder. Rituals designed in my head to prevent death from happening. They lasted for years, obviously I was not taken to therapy but just told I looked increasingly peculiar. One of my rituals was looking to the side whilst praying and blowing on my hands. Yes, I must have looked very peculiar.

I was exhausted, I remember that. The final stage aged 13 was running up and down the stairs in our Victorian house in London whilst the 6pm news was on. This was in an effort to avert a nuclear war between Russia and the US. I had to click the living room light switch on and off an equal amount of times. Sometimes 8, sometimes 16. It had to be an even number and it had to feel right when it was completed. Anyone who has suffered with Obsessive Compulsive Disorder (CBD) knows what I am referring to. There were other rituals but one day I just said to myself, this is enough. So I resisted the urge to engage in my 'safety' rituals. The stress in resisting them gradually diminished. I had not the realization at the time that I had engaged in my own Cognitive Behavioural Therapy program of OCD treatment. I'm only left with obsessive hand washing now, which has come in handy during covid times. Normally if I start washing my hands repeatedly and feel anxious if I have touched something and not washed them, I am aware that I must be feeling stressed about something. It's a bit like having a handy hint to take it easy or reduce stress in some way.

Years later when we were adults my Mother would still feel furious at the idea of mothers being asked to hold their dead baby to say goodbye. She saw it as evil and callous. It felt too cruel to suggest to her that maybe if she had done it she would not have spent the rest of her life in a sort of abstracted state of depression.

My sister is a celebrant, which means she is licensed to act as a non-religious official at funerals. She counsels the family who have lost a loved one. She finds out what really made the person tick. She wanted to do this work because she was fed up with going to funerals where the local Vicar in his/her sermon described a person none of the congregation recognised. The Vicar having gathered together a few pertinent facts and then portrayed the person in a way that was far from the person anyone really knew. So she made it her business and continues to, to really get the family to tell her who this person was and what they loved, found annoying, had a laugh about etc. She has a particular talent of being thoughtful, caring and yet with a no nonsense approach.

My brother-in-law has worked his entire career at a Crematorium in the Midlands. He has a certain gentle care and quiet leadership that makes him especially sensitive to the needs of the people who pass through the chapel. Asking him about his emotional resilience he told me that the little coffins still get him. A bit like an actor who needs to give up if he gets no stage nerves, my brother-in-law had right to the end the respect for those who were being cremated. Whether there was a congregation bursting out of the chapel, or no one there at all, as increasingly he told me people were not. Hospital to crematorium is an increasingly common phenomenon.

So between my brother-in-law and my sister, conversations about the practicalities of death and how the rituals are arranged are never far from the dinner table. Different innovations such as ecological burials in cardboard coffins etc., carbon footprints of cremations, death and how it is managed practically has been in our family from most angles. It perhaps has helped me not feel quite so squeamish about it, nor fear the place where death is dealt with. The crematorium I know best is a gorgeous landscaped place in the middle of wild countryside. It's not creepy at all. Graveyards were much loved by my Mother because she was fascinated by the writing on the gravestones, particularly the Victorian ones. She wasn't bothered about being buried in one herself however, the least bother to everyone left was always her motto.

In the book other cultures and ideas from the past shall be looked at and the stark comparison with how we deal with death in our modern, more secular age shall be looked at. The question I'm fascinated in is are we helping ourselves with new innovative approaches to grieving or are we creating a mental health crisis of anxiety when we feel we have to be our own God?

ACKNOWLEDGEMENTS

I should like to thank the many people who have contributed material to this book and have helped inform and humanize this work. I should like to thank my Dad, Maurice Laurence Reginald Isaac who inspired me to write and who always viewed politics with the benefit of historical premise and pragmatism. He never really said what his view was as such, about anything, he just gave examples from history to refute an argument. It encouraged me to look at politics and all issues in the same way.

I would also like to thank my son, Rupert Bennett and daughter Henrietta Bennett for encouraging me to keep going with this project and believing in me. And to my husband Brien, who knew when I needed to retire and pursue some of my dreams. He has kept the home fires burning whilst I pursue my writing and standup comedy. He never quite knows what's coming next and is usually the last to know!

CONTENTS

CHAPTER 1

HOW DEATHS OF FAMOUS PEOPLE HAVE BEEN TREATED

It's a morbid subject death.   One that has become increasingly sanitized in our modern world. Expressions allude to it. We use euphemisms instead. A passing. When did she pass? We lost him. She has passed over the rainbow bridge. He was taken from us. This use of the passive tense gives a strong feeling of wrong doing, of injustice, as if we have been cheated in some way. In the last year alone there has been a litany of outpourings due to the sad loss of some talented artists. David Bowie, the artist formerly known as Prince, George Michael. With their deaths came expressions of anger, loss, blame even universal meanings such as the year.   Fans searched for links in conspiracies, astrological trends, to explain away what, to me seems to be simple science. There was a search for a meaning that could put a name to their emotion, that could express what that artist meant to them. Through the intrigue and the story in some sense they could keep their hero alive. They could give them an immortality that simple biological facts might deny them. Whilst the artists' brilliance should never be diminished or forgotten, all three had well documented drug addictions during their lives which one would presume massively affected their life expectancy. In deed the old style of death by drugs, Kurt Cobain, the Doors' front man James Morrison, where there was some honesty about the situation, somehow added to their mystique.

Jimi Hendrix died on September 18th 1970 aged 27 in London. This started the cult of the '27' the age where so many brilliantly talented stars die. The idea is still prominent in the media to this day. There was intrigue surrounding his death. The broad strokes were that he had spent his last day primarily with Monika Dannermann, his girlfriend, and others. He had taken an upper, smoked hashish and possibly drunk some red wine before being fetched from a house party by Monika who was determined he return with her to her apartment in Notting Hill.   There he took 9 Vesparax sleeping tablets (18 times the recommended dose). By morning an ambulance was called and they found the door open, curtains drawn and Jimi covered in dried vomit all over his face and body. He was taken to St Mary Abbots hospital where he was announced deceased at 12.45pm.   A post mortem concluded that the cause of death was aspiration on his own vomit and death by asphyxia while intoxicated with barbiturates. Further to his death there was a lifetime of conflicting accounts and criticism was levelled against Monika Dannermann, that she constructed an entire career and identity around Jimi having been the one 'with' him at the time of his death. Her life ended in suicide much later.

It was only two weeks later on October 4th, 1970, in this crazy drug fueled era of brilliance that Janis Joplin died aged 27. Janis died of acute heroin and morphine intoxication due to an apparent overdose. In respect as to her wishes (who details their death wishes at this age?), her body was cremated and her ashes were dropped from a light aircraft along the Northern Californian coastline near Stintson Beach. She had also wanted 2500 USD to be set aside for her wake at which the Grateful Dead and other performers would provide entertainment. Her 200 guests received invites which read 'Drinks are on Pearl' (Pearl was her nickname). The instructions and arrangements are an indication of how artists would become concerned not just with their earthly fame, but how they might be remembered. That whilst trying to control their emotions and creativity, however unsuccessfully, with drugs and alcohol they also would try and control how their death would be handled. It might be argued that this was the start of the 'me era'. The ego wanting to control all aspects of life both whilst alive and managing their death and the grieving process. There had been quite a circus with both the death of Jimi Hendrix and the death of Janis Joplin and Pamela Morrison (Jim Morrison's wife) and indeed his own family supported her in how she chose to deal with the death of her husband in 1971. Again aged 27.

Rolling Stone on August 5th 1971 gave this obituary:

James Douglas Morrison, Poet: Dead at 27
Ben Fong-Torres

Jim Morrison, a man who sang, wrote and drank hard as lead singer of the Doors, has died – peacefully – at the age of 27. Morrison's death, despite (and because of) strategic efforts on the part of his wife Pamela and friends, was shrouded in mystery.

He died in the early morning of Saturday, July 3rd, but it was July 9th, two days after he had been buried in a Paris cemetery, before his manager let word out to the American press.

Bill Siddons, the Doors' manger, explained in a statement:

'The initial news of his death and funeral was kept quiet because those of us who knew him intimately and loved him as a person wanted to avoid all the notoriety and circus-like atmosphere that surrounded the deaths of Janis Joplin and Jimi Hendrix'

...There was no service, and that made it all the better. We just threw some flowers and dirt and said goodbye

...So despite their best efforts rumoured then circulated that actually he was resting and his death was not real.

...Elmer Valentine, owner of the Whisky a Go Go, where the Doors made their first dents as a house band, stayed

close to the band.....'Jim wasn't a doper' Valentine said
'He drank himself to death, but he wasn't a doper'
Ultimately his wife Pamela wanted him to be remembered as a poet in Paris, not as the Doors front man or in the LA madness.

Ironically his resting place has become a place of pilgrimage for Door's fans and his legacy as a rock musician perpetuates. Whatever his wife wanted she achieved at the time of his death, in defiance of the notoriety that other deaths had attracted. After that she had no control over what happened. Fans from all over the world visit his grave in Paris. It is a monument to his rock star status, his early death, aged 27. The mystique of who he might have become. His wife could not manage that side of his death.

In death we lose control. Not just as individuals, but in how people speak about us, refer to us, paint our lives. Our reckoning is no longer just with the almighty, but with the history that we have left on earth. The longer time passes after death, the more possibility there is with changing mores for a life having been deemed extraordinary or brilliant can become ideologically unacceptable or not politically correct. We now see statues of the great pulled down due to imperial past crimes or put up due to historians now interpreting the work of previously unsung heroes as being game changing. History is always alive and remodeled. So are the famous players who have been centre stage.

James Morrison's wife could control his image as best she could, she could remember him as she loved him, she could bury him in the way she wanted him to be buried, but his mourning is up to the rest of the world and his music fans. Their interpretation of what his life meant to them is what matters. That cannot be controlled. In dying it is those left behind who mourn. If you are famous it is not just the close family who have ownership of the emotion. People who have never met you can feel enormous emotions because the person of notoriety meant something to them, touched them in some way in their life and they feel they have the right to mourn them as they see fit.

Conspiracy theorists rush to question why in 2016 so many great artists died?

A more logical statement might be they had a pretty good run for their money and managed to achieve great works. That often brilliant creative talents are tortured souls and that drug taking is common amongst successful artists. But rational statements in these times are seen almost as heretical. In deed such is the fear of death in our times and a desire for mastery over it, that we are in a constant state of hysteria surrounding it. This book will look at the meaning of death in diverse social settings. How the concept is managed and how we come to terms with the one thing

in life we still cannot avoid. From the moment we are
created we hurtle day by day towards our end.

CHAPTER 2

WHY WE CANNOT NAME DEATH

The difficulty with naming death seems to be a cross cultural phenomenon. She has passed, he was taken. The use of the passive and the use of the past tense gives us a sort of gap in between what has happened and gives it a more mystical, elegant tone. Politicians use this linguistic device to distance themselves from scandal, screw ups or unpopular policy. By phrasing unwanted news with linguistic distance, the reality is somehow softened. Rough edges taken off. But much as I cannot tolerate the use of euphemisms for sexual body parts, nor can I in relation to death and disease. So if you are talking about a penis then call it that. Not manhood, or willy. If you are talking about your vagina then do so. Not, in the dreadful 50 shades trilogy, 'my goddess'. If something has a serious function and or action it should be named as such and not wrapped up in code. Is it to avoid offence or that it sounds too blunt or shocking? It surely avoids dubious connotations or positive connotations.

The use of euphemisms are descriptives that add judgement to a point of fact. To return to the body parts. A vagina is a vagina. A goddess ramps up the functional animal part to something to be revered and honoured. While the lad use of a 'gash' sounds self-serving, a useful device to enter. Derogatory as if a slip of a knife ended up with a gash. Similarly, with the penis. A penis is a penis. His manhood suggests that it is big and that it represents something honourable and upholding. Not a part of the body that you urinate from as well as copulate. An incongruous pairing would be taking your manhood and peeing. The two do not work together. So whilst it is fair to say that looking at anatomical parts and naming them is different to naming an action, there is a continuity there. So the action (living) becomes a different action (dying). A reductive action which cumulates in a death. Which is the final point of action. The living action is finished. So then a different active process takes up and that is of the process of dying and deterioration.

This disengagement from reality, or use of metaphor is also employed when talking about cancer. Susan Sontag was an American writer, filmmaker, philosopher and political activist, 1993 – 2004. She wrote a highly influential paper, "Illness as a metaphor" looking at the comparative traits and assumptions in the portrayal of cancer as opposed to say TB which was considered something of a passionate disease. Partly she theorized because TB consumed the body and a Victorian would lie languidly and pale in bed, whilst cancer attacks bits of a body. Bits which can induce shame. Anal cancer, breast cancer. In avoiding this potential shame people mask the reality with metaphors. There is also some superstitious apportioning of guilt in cancer. Ideas persist, which are not held up by any evidence in scientific research, that if you repress your emotions, if you have had a shock, if you are miserable etc., you lay yourself open to getting cancer. The scientific evidence does not support this. Predominantly cancer appears to be a result of your genetic familial print added to which your lifestyle, what fuel or poison you put in your body.

I was part of a European wide research project (EPIC) looking at genetic versus food in rates of cancer, it was found that some cancers were more prevalent and less prevalent due to dietary factors. Our centre of research was in Strangeways Laboratory in Cambridge, part of the University and the UK Epidemiology centre. There were other centres that we liaised with, in particular Nancy in France. There were fascinating findings and insignificant ones. The epidemiologists got most excited by anomalies. An interesting one was throat cancer which was much more prevalent in a certain area of France, whilst the diet in two areas seemed more or less the same. This baffled the scientists in Cambridge and France, until they realized that in this region in France there was a cultural difference in drinking. In one area Brandy was drunk cold with cheese after a meal. In the other Brandy was heated with a flame to quite a high temperature before drinking. The combination of the alcohol and it been hot pointed to a ritualistic burning of the back of the throat, adding a carcinogenic component causing a specific cancer. (European Prospective Investigation into Cancer and Nutrition epic.iarc.fr).

Susan Sontag was interested in why we need to use metaphors with disease. Why the language needed to be abstracted. And why we classify some diseases in a different way and with different metaphors. So this infuriating use of weapon imagery. She 'fought cancer bravely for three years'. 'She finally lost the fight against cancer'. 'Cancer finally defeated her'. There is a distancing again from illness, from a reality, whilst some element of blame attachment that so long as you fight hard enough or strongly enough and if you hadn't been such in infernal worrier you wouldn't have got this cancer in the first place. Perhaps this is how people make sense of someone's illness? Why her? She was so healthy and so fit and so happily married, etc. Ah but her family had it in their genes. Ah really, phew. This sort of reassurance at a distance, reassuring oneself that it won't be you next. What would happen in previous eras? Surely then it would be given up to God. The community would accept God's will and pray for the ill patient.

Sontag makes the connection that with successive diseases, psychological reasons are given when no physical reason can be found, she says *'Psychologizing seems to provide control over the experiences and events (like grave illnesses) over which people have in fact little or no control:'*

As a psychotherapist I frequently had clients referred to me when a Doctor had exhausted all reasonable clinical investigations. The logic being that there was a psychological reason for the pain. Whilst I could help a hypochondriac, learning to restrict looking up symptoms on the internet etc., I could not help someone with a pain that the Doctor had not found the cause for.

I remember seeing a man for about 8 months for chronic pain in his leg. I tried everything, telling him to work up to jogging again, try and increase exercise gradually, meditate to stop fixating on the pain etc., etc. I found him not to be neurotic, he had never had fears of going out or anxiety attacks. There was no drama in his family situation, although his wife was getting rather fed up of him complaining about his leg. He did dredge up some near adultery years ago, but we decided he hadn't actually gone for it and he retained his love for his wife, so the likelihood of this being some psychosomatic pain due to guilt seemed highly unlikely. His whole approach, personality was very grounded. I kept asking and they've checked everything? Because as far as I can see you're just in a lot of pain. He returned to the hospital. Amazingly the one test they hadn't given him was an x ray and realized he had had a broken leg for a year. Quel surprise it was hurting him to jog. The wisest thing any Doctor or Psychotherapist can do is to listen to their patient. They know far better how their body normally feels and how it is feeling currently.

Sontag goes on to make the connection between our need to control disease as being linked to our need to control death, *'Indeed part of the denial of death in this culture is a vast expansion of the category of illness as such'.*

Ten years later Sontag revised her book to include how HIV and Aids are also negative diseases with blame and shame attached to them. This reassurance to Joe Bloggs that he won't get it that's fine because he's not a homosexual and he doesn't do heroin. She thinks that we are living in an era of medical triumphalism. Before *'.....illnesses were innumerable, mysterious, and the progression from being seriously ill to dying was something normal (not as now, medicine's lapse or failure, destined to be corrected)'.*

The connection between Sontag's ideas about illness and our denial of death is embedded in our cultural norms. We are frightened by something that is outside of our control and we search desperately to escape our inevitable demise.

CHAPTER 3

HOW A SCIENTIST DESCRIBES DEATH

Physical death is when the vital organs no longer work. The digestive and respiratory systems start to shut down as the being gradually dies. A dying person no longer wishes to eat because the digestive track dries and swallowing and chewing becomes laborious and painful. Urinating and defecating then also becomes painful. The circulatory systems slows and fails and pooling of blood may appear under the body or appear like bruises on the upper side of the body. Breathing becomes shallow and as the airways fill with mucous may make a rattle noise.

Once dead then the dead body becomes a vast complex ecosystem. Decomposition begins several minutes after death with a process called autolysis or self-digestion. Soon after the heart stops beating cells no longer have oxygen and their acidity increases as the toxic by-products of chemical reactions start to assimilate within them. Enzymes feast on the cell membranes and then start to leak out as the cell walls break down. The process is started and fastest in the liver which is full of enzymes and in the brain which has the most water content. The process is set at altering speeds throughout the body until all the tissues and organs are involved resulting in broken blood vessels flooding out and settling with gravity at the base of the body.

A previously warmer body temperature reduces to fit its surroundings. Rigor mortis sets in the with the eyelids, jaw and neck muscles working its way south to the trunk of the body and then out to the limbs. The chemical reason for this phenomenon is that whilst living muscle cells contract and relax because of two filamentous proteins called acting and myosin which slide along each other. Once these cells no longer are active the protein filaments lock in place causing the muscles to become rigid and lock the joints.

In the early stages of decay of the body, bacteria is confined to those that naturally survives within the body or on the body with most lying within the gut (which has trillions of bacteria of hundreds, possibly thousands of different species). It is a massive area of research for microbiologists as it believed to be the cause of multiple illnesses and conditions. It is mind blowing to think of the sheer number to account for in a live body, but once dead the microbes change again.

In August 2014 a forensic scientist Gulnaz Javan, Alabama State University, Montgomery and co., published the first study of what they termed 'Thanatomicrobiome' (Thanatos, Greek word for death). She found that most organs in the body do not have microbes when we are alive, but once dead the immune system now redundant, means that they spread through the body without restraint. The basic function is that starting with the gut the body begins to eat itself, the digestive system, the lymph nodes, the liver, spleen, heart and brain. The timings of when the microbes have reached each organ systematically can also help with the timing of when a death has occurred. The last system to be affected are the reproductive organs.

At a facility in Texas, The Southeast Texas Applied Forensic Science Facility, 2009 there is a 9-acre area of wooded land, protected by a 10 foot green barbed wire fence. In 2011, SHSU (Sam Houston State University) placed two dead cadavers there and left them to decay under natural conditions. Once self-digestion is underway and bacteria have started to escape from the gastrointestinal tract, putrefaction begins. This is known as molecular death as the soft tissue is broken down even further into gases, liquids and salts. This action is speeded up once anaerobic bacteria take action. Putrefaction is associated with a marked shift from aeorobic bacterial species which need oxygen to grow, to anaerobic which do not. Tissues are fermented and the sugars that are produced turn into gases, methane, hydrogen sulphide and ammonia. The pressure of the buildup of gas causes blisters to appear all over the skin. Skin then loosens and slips. Eventually the gases and liquefied tissues purge from the body from the anus and other orifices and ripped skin.

Occasionally pressure builds to such an extent that the abdomen bursts open.

In recording timelines of death or decomposition, bloating is a marker as is the shift in the composition of cadaveric bacteria.

Butcheli and Lynne took samples of bacteria from various parts of the bodies at the beginning and end of the bloat stage, extracting bacterial DNA and sequencing it.

Bodies becomes hosts for various necrophagous (dead-eating) insects. When a body starts to purge it becomes fully exposed to its surroundings and it then becomes a dish for microbes, insects and scavengers. Blow files are alerted to a dead body by the foul, sickly sweet odour that is emitted. They have receptors on their antennae and lay their eggs on open orifices and wounds. Within 24 hours these eggs are first stage maggots, then second and finally third stage maggots. This movement of maggots create a lot of heat.

The human body left in soil after time decomposes attracting maggots, flies, insects, animal waste nourishing the ecosystem.

(The above was presented in a programme for the BBC and MOSAIC gave Facebook and social media the right to reproduce the contents)

This is the scientific breakdown of a body in certain conditions. The breakdown changes dramatically in different conditions. In deed reports of frozen bodies found on mountains or glaciers, exemplifies how the process of death is organic. It starts within but is defined in its resolution by the external environment. In the dry heat of Texas summer a body will mummify rather than decompose fully, the skin sticking to the bones rather than slipping. Thus the Egyptians in the pre-dynastic period wrapped their dead in linen and buried them directly in the sand. The heat inhibited microbe activity and burial stopped insects reaching them and so they were well preserved. In attempting to make the afterlife even better for their dead they built tombs with possessions inside them. In fact, this did not protect them from decomposition and so they learnt to embalm and mummification.

In Ancient Egypt the embalmer would first wash the body with palm wine and Nile water, remove the internal organs by an incision on the left hand side of the body and pack them with natron (a naturally occurring salt mixture found in the Nile valley). A hook would be used to pull the brain out through the nostrils and then the entire body would be covered with natron and left to dry for 40 days.

The organs were firstly put in canopic jars, buried alongside the body, later they would be wrapped in linen and then returned to the body. Finally the body itself was wrapped in many layers of linen in preparation for burial.

Embalming in the United States is very popular. An embalmer will use embalming fluid consisting of formaldehyde, methanol and other solvents. It temporarily preserves the body's tissues by linking cellular proteins to each other and fixing them in place. The fluid kills bacteria and prevents them from breaking down the proteins and using them for food. An embalming machine is used to push the embalming fluid through the carotid artery and subclavian vein from the neck. As the fluid goes through the vein system, blood pours out of the incision and in to a sort of gutter and into a skink. It takes about an hour to remove all the blood from an average sized person. Massaging the body whilst this happens helps break up blood clots that might be blocking the passage of the embalming fluid and helps the fluid flow through the body.

The next stage is aspirating the abdomen and sucking fluids out of the body cavity including urine and feces that might still be there. The incision is stitched. The body is wiped down and the face set, hair brushed etc.. The body is redressed and is ready for the funeral.
Embalmed bodies eventually also decompose and the time that takes is also dependent on the outside conditions in which the body is placed.

Bodies are just energy, waiting to be released into the world. The theory of thermodynamics says that energy cannot be created or destroyed, just converted from one form to another.

(Key reference: *Life after death: the science of human decomposition, Mo Costandi, The Guardian, 5 May 2015* under Creative Commons licence)

CHAPTER 4

THE PERVERSION OF DEATH

We addressed earlier the tradition of embalming, a way of preserving the body in its physical exterior presentation. In open casket funerals the dressing of the body is an important part of the ritual where the congregation file past the casket to pay their last respects to the family member or church member. Famous figures in catholic countries are normally presented in an open casket for crowds to pay homage and witness to the death of a leader or famous figure in their country or community. One presumes the preparation of the body has been done with precision and detachment or respect, but being human there is the possibility of human 'failings of respect' or perversion. Their loved one is dead. But here is the very essence of the importance of grief and funerals being about the living and not about the dead is at play. The presentation of the body in a dignified and peaceful way is what is being paid for. To help the family find some comfort. That their last look is not as painful as it might be.

In the DSMV (Diagnostic and Statistical Manual of Mental Disorders Fifth edition published by the American Psychiatric Association) Necrophilia is listed under Paraphilia Not Otherwise Specified. This section includes fetish for particular object or substance.

Psychiatric manuals have viewed Necrophilia as a desire to desecrate and abuse. In the previous testament it might not be as simplistic as that. There might indeed be a plethora of reasons for the desire and the consequent action.

Necrophilia concerns a pathological fascination with dead bodies which frequently results in engaging in some form of sexual activity with them. Despite laws prohibiting this behavior there has been a long history.

Case History

In the suburbs of Chicago lies an unassuming area of middle income, professional houses. A clinic deals with the normal variety of mental issues that arise living and working, commuting often downtown to Chicago. Long hours interrupted by domestic tension, affairs, school issues, drug issues. The normal presenting problems at a counselling service. The service worked with a group of counsellors and therapists who would discuss cases in a group setting for further guidance, problem solving. The same way that most therapists work whether in the states or elsewhere in the developed world. A therapist found herself working with an interesting and sympathetic young man. He was good looking and was one of a family of 5. He had married reasonably young and embarked on having his own family, a dream he had cherished. His wife was a policewoman within the local community. They were well thought of. He was a mortician and he commented on how it was a bit of either a conversation stopper or conversation starter when people first met him. He had sort of fallen into the work having met a man who was in the profession and had persuaded him that with his character and artistry, if he could stomach it, he could make a good living doing this work. And of course it is recession proof. There is always a demand.

So he had trained initially just as a mortician and then as an embalmer. He was proud of his skills. Sadly, his marriage was in trouble. This was his reason for coming to see the therapist. His wife could not see a future with him. He had temporarily (so he hoped), moved out of the family home and was sofa surfing with friends whilst he looked for an apartment he could afford. In reality he was searching for a way to recover his marriage. There were so many issues. He was extremely depressed and full of shame. Often he would cancel his appointments with the therapist at the last minute. The therapist had already flagged up to the group service that she thought he was a suicide risk. Not just because of his extremely poor mental health, but because he had the location and the tools and chemicals and the knowledge to kill himself should he choose to do so. He had not expressly said that he was suicidal, but he had expressed suicidal ideation.

I wish I could just go away and not face any of this. I sometimes just want to disappear. I don't like waking up. It is all too painful.

The therapist developed a trusting relationship with the man. He talked sometimes about his work. Taking pride in how he reduced the visual damage done to a body in a crash, so that the family would not be further traumatized. He explained however that he still left some indication of the wound or crash so that the family could accept why it had happened. That is why the person died. It seemed to the therapist how carefully he considered each body. Each body was not just that. It was a person who had a family who loved them. They would look at the body after he had worked 'his magic' and it would have an eternally lasting effect on their acceptance of the death of their loved one.

It was at this point during the therapy that the therapist realized that the involvement was unhealthy. It was this that the wife was feeling despairing about. It gave her the creeps. She didn't want to hear about his work. She didn't want to have sex with him anymore. He felt lost. He felt unappreciated for his work and unwanted as a man. The only way he was still valued was as a father to his young children. The wife still wanted him to see them regularly.
The therapy continued.

It was an interesting case for the rest of the group to hear about. One of the therapists reflected that their desire to discuss this case so much was slightly indicative of the problem. In that it was rather mawkish. There were many other more humdrum problems that could be discussed. The man who had slept with his personal assistant and was not trying to cover it up to his wife. He was trying to decide which way to go and if he wanted to be married.

The adolescent who was smoking too much weed, but felt it was his only way of controlling the anxiety he had experienced since he was 12 and had changed schools. No these run of the mill therapeutic encounters did not fascinate and wet the appetite as much as the mortician.

Whether this influenced the therapist, acknowledging this salacious interest, it was hard to decide. In therapy there is transference and countertransference seen as an invisible emotional connection and reaction between patient and therapist. As the mortician was describing his personal signature with dead bodies, the therapist asked what he meant? Well he explained. Any mortician knows the work of someone else. They leave a signature as it were. Like watch makers work in such a way that another specialist on opening the watch could name who the specialist was. An artisan who leaves their mark on a Rolex watch. They individualise it. So here there was a sort of god complex. Not only affecting the grieving of the family, but also claiming the body in some way for himself. Clearly he was not alone in this, as evidenced by his reference to the other morticians who leave their signature.

He explained that whenever he worked on a lady, he would leave a trail of violets on their décolletage. A true artist. But as he described this his eyes moved to the young therapist's breasts and she felt a sexual buzz shoot through her body. It was at that point that she feared what was at the root of the marital problem. That in fact his wife suspected that his interest in the female bodies was perverse. The therapist chose not to divulge this latest feeling to the group. She feared that by doing so the work and solution could be damaged. Even that a criminal process could be instigated. So rather than acknowledge it directly, she started to work on why his wife was so uncomfortable? What could he do to start helping his wife feel safer. Eventually the penny had firmly, if invisibly dropped. He decided to never work alone in the Funeral Parlour again. In other words he would not be put in temptation's way again. He would only work during the day, never at night as he done so before. He would never ring his wife from the Funeral Parlour. This used to make her feel more comfortable. He would concentrate more on hobbies that he and his wife could both enjoy without mention of his work, or her work. The therapist tentatively stepped around the unspoken but acknowledged the issue and in doing so stopped the behavior. The marriage recovered. At the end of therapy the patient cried. He said he had been in such a bad place and she had unconditionally believed in him and his ability to get back with his wife.

The extent of the patient's god complex, his sense of omnipotence and even indecency one will never know. But the therapist believed he was trying to find his destroyed self-esteem through his work.

In this case study there are many questions. Was the therapist's hunch correct? It was resolved and a barrier to harm was achieved through brain storming with the patient as to how to work out how to work more professionally and with more boundaries in place that would comfort his wife and make her able to trust him again. But there is a wider philosophical question. To what extent can a human play god? The case history is reminiscent in its content of the obsession that grows with a serial killer. Leaving their mark. Wanting to take control not over the body but the message to the living that it was he who had been there. In the case of the mortician clearly he was not responsible for killing the person, so there is not a crime. But the subsequent behavior is evocative of a serial killer. And what if a mortician is a necrophiliac? That does not harm the body, if one makes an assumption that the body is dead. It no longer holds any function, except to deteriorate at a rapid speed, depending on the environment it is left in. If no one knows that a body has been defiled does it matter? Has a crime been committed? In nine US states there are no laws that address necrophilia.

On the basis of if a tree falls down in a forest and no one is there, does it make a sound? A similar argument could follow that if no one witnesses the act and the person is indeed dead, then no one is hurt. But equally there is a visceral emotional reaction to the thought of such an act. But is it repulsion at the perpetrator? compassion for the victim? or for their family? The family should after all feel that if they are paying quite a price for a service to show their loved ones as they want to remember them, that to desecrate that body would be an appalling crime of violation. Violation of the corpse and violation of their trust.

But with a logical and unemotional brain it could be argued that if the body is just that, dead matter, there should no need to feel compassion for the victim as they are not a victim. Herodotus (c.484-425 BC) in his Histories said that beautiful Egyptian women were not embalmed immediately after death, but only after several days, as an embalmer had been caught having sex with a recently dead woman. In this instance there was probably a less frequent availability of women for sex. It was not the days of Tinder. Sexual frustration and mystification could be a rationale for the embalmer taking the liberty of a fresh body. The implication, by Herodotus, is that a few days later that temptation would not be inviting. The smell would be repellent.

This 'availability concept and ownership' seems to fit with Herschel Prins (criminologist) who reported that if a girl in Central Europe died prior to the wedding day, the groom could still have the marriage day by copulating with the body. This arrangement seems likely to be concerned with material gain to claim a dowry, or to claim conjugal rites even after death.

In times of war rape and pillaging is a common theme. A combination of dominance, power and opportunity. Considering the numbers of men who have engaged in this activity, it begs the question whether there is a true psychological rapist profile, or if indeed when the structures of society allows, many men are capable of rape and of killing. Following this theory, during the 18th century conflict in Peru between Tupac Amaru and Colonial forces, rebels had sex with dead women. (*Walker, Charles F. (2014) The Tupac Amru Rebellion Harvard University Press p.10*)

Necrophilia was reported in subsequent conflicts during the Moroccan War of 1919-1926 and during the Rwandan genocide. And if a lone man goes against the moral vacuum, then they endanger themselves in their social grouping. A Chinese Man was killed during the Nanking Massacre for refusing to have sex with a dead woman.   Presumably his sense of honour and independent thought was threatening to the others who were behaving like animals. *(An, Armando (2005)/ The brutal holocaust: Japan's World War II atrocities and their aftermath. A1 Pub. P.75)*

So when there is war, different social norms prevail. It is not, one assumes, that overnight hundreds of men developed fetishes or psychiatric disorders, but the law of the jungle allowed them to behave in a way they may never have desired to before. Certainly never been allowed to. And in a mob mentality a sort of collective fetishism and anger might explain their behavior.

So it can be determined that it is not a one hat fits all approach to Necrophilia.

Another side of Necrophilia is associated with finding a victim and murdering her in order to provide the body for the sexual act. The interest in having access to a dead body is so powerful that a person is prepared to kill in order to gain the body. Earle Nelson (1987 – 1928) was an American serial killer who mainly preyed on landladies (previously unknown to him and therefore could not be linked to him). He would carry a bible which would make the woman feel safe with him. Once he had gained their trust, he would strangle them and then have intercourse with their body. (*Gribben, Mark "Earle Leonard Nelson: The Dark Strangler" Crime Library   archived   from   the original,http:www.trutv.com/library/crime/serial_killers /history/earle_nelson/1.html) on 2010-10-13. Retrieved October 10, 2013.)*

In the above case is an example of the strong drive to get the body to copulate with. The Necrophilic behavior is not opportunist, it is functional. He finds a live, breathing woman and murders her to have ability to have sexual action on her body. Interestingly, and one which shall be addressed later, such is our secular society that a man clutching a bible these days would be more likely to engender fear of a weirdo in a woman, rather than the badge of trust.

A more recent high profile necrophilia case/s was purported to be engaged in by Jimmy Savile (1926-2011). Broadmoor staff members claimed that Savile had told them that he engaged in necrophilac acts with the corpses in their mortuary in Leeds. Savile was good friends with the chief mortician who gave him near unrestricted access. *(Halliday, Josh (26 June 2014) 'Savile told hospital staff he performed sex actions on corpses in Leeds mortuary'. The Guardian. Retrieved 18 June 2017)*

This perversion was in addition to his abuse of sick children who had no means of defending themselves or in some ways being animated. Particularly reports emerged of children with spinal injuries who he had access to. Jimmy Saville had the ability and was aided in his access to paralysed children and corpses and to brag about it, with no fear. He had a power complex, he felt he was untouchable. Partly because he raised such vast sums of money in charity to fund the very hospitals in which he abused his victims. He could somehow seduce people in power, gatekeepers with bribes of vast amounts of money that he raised. Those in power were either in denial, closing their eyes to the unimaginable and disbelief in addition to not wanting to be blamed for losing thousands of pounds in fundraising projects that he spearheaded throughout his career. So the necrophiliac Jimmy Savile was a narcissist. He gave everyone the creeps but he wafted through high society servicing his twisted needs.

A long line of serial killers did not just kill to satisfy a sexual desire with a corpse, but repeatedly raped a woman and then carried on the sexual act once they were corpses. In these instances, it would seem that the initial action was wrapped up in rape and domination and pain and that their excitement continued after the body only existed. Does this qualify as a true necrophilia? It seems likely that the motivation here is for domination, fear and power over a live woman and that the death is part of that whole process. However, Gary Ridgway (1949) was both a serial killer and necrophilia. His killing involved raping sex workers and teenage runaways, strangling them, leaving their bodies in overgrown and forested areas of Kings County and returning to engage in sexual activity with the corpses. So here the immediate action of the rape and murder was not immediately followed by necrophilia. It was a plan. He wanted to leave the bodies to be returned to.

If you are confused by my tenuous logic, it is because I am trying to place necrophilia as more than a one dimensional fetish or perversion or sickness. I am evaluating case histories that have different causal origins. It is not simple. The murderers somehow confuse the issue. A bit like a pedophile murdering a child. The desire for the child is the original driver. The murder is to stop them telling. It does not seem a logical desire for the children to be murdered, but more an act of self-preservation for the offender. So in this sense a purist necrophiliac, if that is not a contradiction in terms, maybe is someone driven by a desire to copulate or perform sexual acts on a non-communicative, uncritical, non-judgmental vessel. They need access to corpses. Bodies historically have been dug up and of course people working with dead bodies have the means and the opportunity.

Jack Pemment writes in Psychology Today an article called 'The Appeal of Necrophilia' which highlights the issue that is being referenced.

Spurious accounts and interest does not help at look at why these people do what they do and it does not point to one cause. As Jack comments:

'......not all necrophilia behavior involves committing homicide'

In 2009, Aggrawal proposed 10 categories of necrophilia. These classifications escalate from 1 to 10 in increasing increments to where the corpse is the only trigger for the sexual excitement. This is what I have been alluding to.
Jack continues with a new approach of where does this interest in death start?

Death is the end of everyone's lives clearly. Religions on the whole attempt to explain death, life after death, as a way of reassuring the living. Death can be associated with great comfort. They are now at peace, suffering is gone. He points out that the grieving process never really ends. Years later we all know the moment when we say, 'ah Dad would have loved this' or conversely, 'do you remember when Mum said this'. They live on in daily memories, hidden, spoken, copied.

Jack is not suggesting that our ongoing conversation with the dead, our reference to the dead means we are all going to become necrophiles. But his point is there could be:

'A pivotal moment when the comfort somebody obtains from thinking about death or the dead, progresses to thinking death and the dead can be recreated for future

happiness. If this breach is made, it might only be exploratory at first, through fantasy, but steadily progress to unhealthy and even illegal behaviours'

That seems a bit of a leap. But certainly death, indeed illness was to some extent fetishized in the Victorian era. Jack talks about our need for intimacy in our DNA. He states that necrophilia stems from the need to have an unresisting partner. Possibly a non-judgmental partner.

'This also goes for the need not to be hurt or let down, or perhaps the fear of being unable to produce a reciprocal orgasm during intercourse. And as morbid as it is to think about, it is easy to be intimate with a corpse because there is no emotional or social work involved, perhaps similar reasons as to why some people, for at least temporary moments in their lives, turn to sex dolls'

There are some elements of explanation in this argument, but to liken our need as humans for intimacy to correlate with being with a corpse, seems to mistake a masturbatory action with what most people would think of in terms of intimacy. A crush, an enjoyment of someone's personality, a hormonal reaction when you smell them, when they laugh, that giddy feeling when you fancy someone or more still when you fall in love with someone. How can this human intimacy, which is our evolutionary specialty, be linked to sex with a corpse?

For a corpse is a body, not a live laughing, breathing, funny, interesting, talking human being. It is lifeless. So whilst it may well be that the driver for the person who acts on a compulsion to have sex with a corpse may be inclined due to problems with expectations, this surely cannot be described in terms of a human need for intimacy.

Jack reasons that even a corpse is still human. This is central to the concept that has been discussed. To what extent does a body after death still be viewed as human?

Jack Pemment is a neuroscience graduate from the University of Mississippi. He explores the neurobiology of criminal behavior and personality disorders.
Online: Blame the Amygdala

CHAPTER 5

STILL BORN AND BRIEF LIVES

Stillbirths, despite the statistics being dramatically fewer than in history, sadly remain a reality for many families. A miscarriage is defined as the loss of a baby before the 20th week of pregnancy and a stillbirth the loss of a baby at or after 20 weeks of pregnancy. Within that definition there is a further classification of an early stillbirth between 20 and 27 weeks of pregnancy. A late stillbirth occurs between 28 and 36 weeks of pregnancy. And a stillbirth occurs between 37 and more completed weeks of pregnancy.

Stillbirth in the US still affects about 1 in 160 births.

In the 19th century in the Victorian era there were 149 deaths per 1000 from birth to the first year of life. The most vulnerable time for a newborn baby has always been the first 24 hours. With each hour a newborn baby survives the better the chances of their survival. It is hard to compute how many babies were born still born or had brief lives as there was poor registration. For example, in France, Belgium and the Netherlands under Napoleonic Code in the 19th and early 20th centuries, 'any deaths occurring before registration (in practice up to three to five days after birth) could be considered stillborn, and therefore discounted from infant mortality statistics'.

A study by, *Cambridge Group for the History of Population and Social Structure on 'The relationship between stillbirth and early neonatal mortality: evidence from eighteenth century London' Romola Davenport*

The Introduction states that the first day of life is the most dangerous. Mortality declines from the point of birth throughout the first days of life and generally declines into late adolescence. The parish records of St Martins in the Fields are used to look at the mortality rate of stillborn and early neonatal mortality in 18th century London. An important aspect of the study and statistics shows an uncertain recording of stillborns, registered possibly as such due to the difference in price of stillborn burial and the burial of a baptized infant. The records were detailed however in the Sexton's burial books, which recorded the cost and other details of the burial in the parish. They recorded the name, street address, sex, cause of death and exact age of the deceased. In an infant's in days, weeks and months whilst both burials of stillborns and abortives were recorded in detail. It seems likely that many early neonatal deaths were buried as stillborn. At this time the age of a baby was taken from its baptism date, which is an important measure. The study seems to assume that many early neo-natal deaths were recorded as stillborns. The cheapest burials were abortives. As the burial of a stillborn and a Chrisom

Child (a child who dies before baptism) was the same, it seems that it may have been noted from the point of view of stigma rather than an economic rationale.

There also may have been a legal confusion about how to differentiate between an actual stillborn and an infant born who takes a few breaths but is not viable. To avoid charges of murder it would be important for all that a non-viable baby would be recorded as stillborn rather than investigation into the reason for death.

One of the entries described is a 'Chrisom Child' aged four hours, but described as stillborn at burial. The study is interested in how differently deaths were recorded both in the workhouse and in more affluent parishes in London, to see to what extent health practices changed and whether social status influenced recording practices. From the position of this work, the question remains in the upcoming personal testament from Lilian, *'if we do not notate and bear testament to every life and death, then who are any of us?'*

Stillborn babies and babies with brief lives have of course a tremendous effect on a family and on the mother and father, not to mention siblings. I have included two quite complex testaments of brief lives which in their different context and acknowledgement of the loss of babies provide a wealth of psychological inspiration and understanding as to how as humans we process grief.

Anecdotal Testimony

Rosie was awaiting her first baby. She was full of excitement at the prospect that her and her husband Carl would be parents. The pregnancy had progressed well and Rosie was just waiting until the baby was born before she bought the crib and the buggy. It was a superstitious thing. On her last scan appointment, at 38 weeks, the process seemed to take longer than normal. Nothing was said then. The following day Rosie and Carl got a phone call from the head of the natal unit. Could they come in for an appointment. Yes, sure when? Now. Oh ok, but its Saturday and we are on our way to Metz. Now please, we will talk through a couple of issues, but don't worry we can sort it out.

Arriving at the hospital Rosie was aware that they were the only people in the waiting room. When the Doctor came in and touched her, Rosie says she felt a spirit shoot through her and she knew that she was going to lose her daughter. You can tell me whatever you like, but I felt it and I knew there and then. Rosie fell on the floor sobbing, the Doctor reassured her, we can do something.

The problem they had seen was the heart of their baby was back to front and in Luxembourg they did not have the expertise to operate on the baby as soon as she was born. But they did in Brussels and so they would arrange to have the baby on the Monday in Brussels. The Doctor had also seen the brain was swollen, but thought this could either be a brain issue or to do with the heart not functioning properly.

Carl had gone into automatic processing mode. He was ringing a brain specialist he knew who was on a conference in Singapore, but he was prepared to fly back if necessary to help with the baby in Brussels as and when.

There was so much support for the couple. But such was Rosie's upset and sadness that the shock sent her into labour. So the baby was born screaming and bawling, very much alive, but lasted only a short time out of the womb Rosie felt as if she was above her body watching everything, like a movie in slow motion. The medical staff said that they had resuscitated her twice but she had stopped breathing again, what did they want Rosie to do? Rosie said 'keep trying'. Subsequently when the death was confirmed, Rosie was sedated, such was the level of her distress. Carl could not bring himself to hold the baby, it was too traumatic.

The following day the Doctor asked Rosie if she would like to hold the baby to say goodbye. Rosie, a strong Baptist Christian, believed it's important to let a soul go. And so as the mother she needed to hold her baby and let her go to heaven, to give her permission if you like. And so she was led to an underground room in the hospital, which had been lit by a hundred candles. There was a nun with the baby, who had been dressed. Rosie held the baby and saw the baby's face, who looked very like Carl. To this day she remembers her baby's face. She believes that holding her baby helped her to grieve. For her it was important that she could let her baby go to heaven and have peace.

Each year Rosie and her family put a bauble on the Christmas Tree with the baby's name on, as testament to being part of the family even though she is in heaven.

The testimony above recognizes a grief that is processed partly through religious belief and partly through ritual. The religious conviction of Rosie helps her to truly believe that her baby is in heaven and that gives her peace and meaning. She acknowledges that the years help with the pain. But the ritual of the bauble on the Christmas Tree helps Carl and the rest of the family. The life, however short lived of the baby, is acknowledged in the family and she is represented by the placing of the bauble on the Christmas Tree. However, many years have passed, her place is still set in the family history and is acknowledged by the brothers who never knew her, but know she existed and is part of their history. In the next testament, a 40-year complex grief is described.

Anecdotal Testimony

Lilian was only 10 years old when she discovered a family secret through 'happenstance'. She was part of a family consisting of two much older brothers, her eldest brother then 18, James and her other brother Simon then 17. Whether by virtue of the age gap, her being a girl, Mum being busy and Dad being emotionally unavailable and a doer not a talker, Lilian had always felt as if she was a sort of 'alien' in her family. She felt as if she didn't fit. As a consequence of this she sought belonging in other families and with other figures who represented alternatives to her own flesh and blood. It was with one such attachment figure, an elderly lady who lived next door to her family and who she saw as a Grandma figure, who 'let the cat out of the bag'.

Lilian was looking around her neighbour's bedroom and caught sight of a very old photo of her neighbour holding a baby. 'Who is this?' she asked, and the neighbor said that it was in fact her baby who sadly died when she was a few days old. It was very sad, but your Mum knows about that doesn't she? Because of course the same thing happened to her? Lilian was shocked. She went home and immediately asked her Mum what this was about? Did she have a baby? What was the truth? And her Mum said yes it was true. She had had a baby who she had named

Caroline. The boys had been born at home with no problem but with this birth the midwife was concerned as it was breach. The Doctor who signed off for the homebirth to go ahead disagreed that it was breach and so the homebirth was authorized against the midwife's better judgement. Caroline was born and the eldest boy came in to meet his little sister in the middle of the night. The baby was put in a cot drawer, part of the chest of drawers and was tragically found deceased by the midwife the following morning. The baby was taken in the drawer with Lilian's mother to the hospital. Her mother was not allowed to hold the baby. At hospital her mother was sedated due to distress and left in a room whilst the baby was taken away in the drawer. Later the Doctors confirmed that the baby had been pronounced dead due to cot death. Lilian's father took his wife home. The drawer was returned to the family by the hospital a week later. Over the next year Lilian's mother had another pregnancy which resulted in an early miscarriage. The Doctor said her family seemed complete and she should return to work as a scientist in a laboratory. This she did. A year later Lilian was conceived and born with no incident. Lilian maintained a belief that her mother had never mourned her elder sister. That the family had never spoken about it but had ironically had 'stuck their grief in a drawer' not to be opened again.

Such was Lilian's sense of disenfranchisement from her own family, her own parents, that she cajoled and tried countless times to get more information from her mother about what had happened. Her father has only ever once acknowledged the existence of her older sister and her death. 40 years on Lilian still felt she did not have closure regarding her sister's death. There were too many gaps in her knowledge to make sense of the story. Her parents had reiterated countless times that it was too painful to talk about and it was done, nothing could be achieved by looking back on it. Could Lilian not just leave it well alone. But Lilian felt as if she was carrying the burden of the grief by her mere existence. It was if the pain had been so much for her Mother that to open her heart to Lilian fully would be too threatening a reality. So Lilian pressed on and contacted a woman who ran an online company called 'Brief Lives'. She ran it out of her experience of ill managed grief after still born babies or babies who had had a 'brief life'.

Lilian gave her what sparse information she had. Within a week the owner of the website company had found out Caroline's actual birth date, her death certificate, the hospital that she and her Mother had been taken to (even this her mother had blocked out of her memory). She had found out that Caroline had been cremated and that the remains had been scattered in a memory garden in a crematorium in Ruislip, North West London. Her mother agreed to go with her to the crematorium and together they walked in the memory garden and looked at some of the plaques that families had recently placed there. They looked at the flowers growing there and knew this was where Caroline had been laid to rest. Lilian was not sure if her Mum found any resolution that day, but she did. Lilian had felt her whole life that she needed to pay testament to her older sister who had not survived. Whether this is survivor guilt, or if she felt such guilt that her Mother had had to go through such loss, even Lilian is unsure. But it felt like a long process that she had now completed to the best of her ability. The pain that her family endured by not talking about the loss and not holding the baby, she believes passionately is something that mothers should be encouraged to do. She has devoted much of her working career supporting the NCT's grief guidance for mothers and fathers of still born and babies with SIDS. To hold them, have photos taken of them, as evidence and part of storing memories that can be revisited. *'If these babies' lives are not documented, then who are any of us?'* she poignantly remarked.

As a note re the baby in the drawer, in the past people often lived in smaller houses and might not have a separate room for the baby, or desired to have the baby close by for feeding. So they often put the baby in a drawer next to the bed. In Finland there was a concept for a 'baby box' where they were introduced by the government in 1938, firstly aimed at low-income pregnant women and subsequently for all. Uptake of the box in Finland is near 95 percent. The baby box has a little mattress in the bottom and becomes the baby's first bed. The box includes bodysuits, a sleeping bag, outdoor gear, bathing products for the baby, nappies bedding and a small mattress. In order to get the maternity box, the pregnant mother had to visit a Doctor or a pre-natal clinic before their 4th month of pregnancy. It helped register all pregnant women with the welfare state. At the introduction of the box Finland was a poor country with a high mortality rate for babies, 65 out of 1,000 babies died. But the figures rapidly declined after the introduction of the baby box. Babies used to sleep in the same bed as their parents and it was recommended that they stopped, says Panu Pulma, professor in Finnish and Nordic History at the University of Helsinki, including the baby box as a bed meant people started to let their babies sleep separately from them and reduced SIDS (Sudden Infant Death Syndrome).

The subsequent child after the loss of a sibling is thought to be at a risk of psychopathology 'the replacement child syndrome'. This was first described by Cain and Cain in 1964 in an effort to work through the complex emotional paradigm of replacing a lost infant with another one. The work suggested that there would be emotional consequences for both the parents and the child and including having 'emotionally unavailable parents'. A description of the substitute child forming 'a self-identity in the shadow of another identity' *(Legg, 1976)*. Latterly this assumption has been challenged as a clinical myth *(Groud and Romonoff, 2000)*. More contemporary theories discuss grief as a reconstruction in which their world is changed irretrievably. Constructivists suggest the existence of processes, whilst 'stage like' theories suggest normative patterns and paths *(Neimeyer, 2010)*.

Perinatal loss and stillborn loss risk not grieving for their loss as it is an ambiguous loss, they struggle to know how to grieve for an unknown child. They also are faced with internal pressure and external social pressure as to whether or not to replace the child. Although some quantative findings indicate pathological issues with attachment problems *(Hughes, 2001)* and replacement child syndrome *(Turton et al, 2009)* for the subsequent child following a stillbirth. The studies suggest an ongoing relationship with the deceased infant may be part of a healthy grieving *(Klass, Silvermen & Nickman, 1996, Rosenblannt, 1996)*.

Qualitative methodology is especially appropriate when one views grief as a reconstruction of experience. Rosie's approach to her loss of her baby is brought to mind. She constructed her grief in a religious context where she had some agency. She held her baby and prayed for her safe delivery into heaven and eternal life. Her husband, not blessed with religious conviction, could get on board with the construction of a memory in the form of the bauble dedicated to their daughter.

Their daughter has a place in the family tree, literally on the family Christmas tree, and their family have therefore made their own construct of healthy grief and a place for their daughter in their family system, however brief her moment in life was.

CHAPTER 6

HOLLYWOOD

From the very start of time, or as early as history has been recorded, humans have attempted to bury, burn, keep their dead for a number of reasons. For sanitary reasons, for religious reasons and for reasons of that very unscientific principle, love.

In Hollywood, in starville, when you have reached the peak of your fame and adoration, when you have been able to seduce whoever you want to, when you have bought every kind of house and car you could imagine, you eventually come to the conclusion that you can only be in one living room at a time, normally with one woman or one man. So then your hopes settle on a higher aspiration.

Maslow's hierarchy of needs is the theory in psychology put forward by Abraham Maslow in 1943 'A Theory of Human Motivation'. Basic needs are at the bottom of the triangle. The more you satisfy all the needs of hunger, shelter, sexual satisfaction and procreation you move on to higher aspiration of belonging and self-esteem, and at the top of the pyramid you search to achieve self-actualisation. So this highest form can take on many forms. The betterment of society, philosophical pursuits, religious and spiritual enlightenment. Plato in 'The Last Days of Socrates' described how Socrates believed that if you had spent most of your life only satisfying your bodily needs then your spirit would not exist after death. Conversely if you had spent most of your life concentrating on your spiritual journey, that the spiritual side of you would be so strong that even though the body died, the spiritual force would carry on. This idea is the cornerstone of most religions and part of a moral voice in most societies. The body is just a tool, the mind is our strength, our virtue our machine to do good with. This concept is at the foundation of Eastern Philosophy and Buddhism. And goodness doesn't Hollywood love Buddhism.

Psychological growth is heavily influenced by this idea of the higher being as the answer to all known problems. It's a hard principle to work on for a person working two jobs and trying to feed their kids. They are far too busy working and clearing up after their children to have time or even the inclination to think about their higher individual purpose. Sit and turn the TV off and the radio off. Have no distractions. Eat mindfully. Savour each mouthful. Look at the colour of the food. Etc., etc. A Buddhist monk may have the time and inclination to do this, but for a busy working Mum, trying to feed her kids, at the same time as answering the phone and helping with homework? But this is possibly the beauty of being further down the food chain. There is no time for existential crisis or people surrounding you and building up your ego. Buddhist concepts give a person a way of living to satisfy their personal needs and those of the 'universe', whilst religions such as Islamic or Christianity concentrates on a book of rules made up by someone else, that is controlled by a preacher of some sort and enforced. The busy man gives up his problems to God, to someone else. A book tells him what he should be doing and he prays to his preacher for forgiveness for his shortcomings. It's like being parented and you give up your problems to someone else who is far better at taking care of them than yourself on your own. It is much easier to lie in bed and pray before you go to sleep than to attempt to block out the real world and concentrate on one aspect in a vain attempt to be your own God. Catholics can go to confession and be given a prescription of penance and prayer by the priest. The dilemma and guilt is taken away as the believer is told how to atone. In an increasing secular and ego driven society the pressure of being the answer to all problems in life has added a burden that humans have previously not encountered.

Studies in Sierra Leone, ravaged by tragedies, found that individual psychological stress was low despite multiple tragedies. Their answer was that it was God's will. So by handing over all responsibility to this higher being there was no guilt or self- blame. It was quite literally out of their hands. God's will had been done and as believers they had to accept it. This belief system, central to societies and cultures since the evolution of man, must be central to our mental health. If we as mere man start trying to take on responsibility for life and death and all meaning then surely we will not be able to withstand the complexity of the responsibility that it entails. In reference to the earlier testament of Rosie, she was able to give up her grief to God and allow her baby girl to be lifted up to heaven, such was her belief as a Baptist Christian.

So to get back to Hollywood. The stars that have everything then become hooked on meaning. Meaning of life, meaning of death, meaning of their existence. How to take control of it and make sense of it? After all they have now become bored with taking care of every other part of their life and they realise that if you have experienced everything then nothing much gives you a kick anymore. And so there is an obsession with eternity in Hollywood. Because despite following diet regimes, getting plastic surgery, paying for expensive anti-ageing treatments, drinking their own urine as in Madonna's case, they realise through experience that fame and money does not make them immune to illness and death. So there is a plethora of films which deal with the fantasy of eternity. 'Always' is a romantic comedy about a flyer who speaks to his lover and friends from beyond the grave, 'Defending Your Life' is a witty comedy set in Judgement City where newly deceased people have to prove that they are capable of moving from fear to love, 'Dragonfly' is a film in which a doctor discovers the gifts hidden in death, 'A Ghost

Story' is a moral fable about letting go, 'Ghost Town' is a comic fantasy, 'Heaven Can Wait' deals with death, immortality, and destiny. 'Hereafter' is a serious piece about the human desire to know more about the afterlife. 'The Sixth Sense' is a supernatural thriller about a young boy who can communicate with the dead. 'What Dreams May Come' is about a man who practices compassion for his soulmate. This is just a snapshot. This subject is something of an obsession in Hollywood and it is my conjecture that they really are searching for an answer and the afterlife plots give them a promise of possibility that it's really going to be ok. With so much power at their fingertips it's unbearable for them to think something is out of their control. And the afterlife is definitely not under their control. Even the possibility is not under their control. It evokes fear. And whilst the main theme of the stories are all about releasing control to the universe and understanding that some things in life cannot be controlled; inevitably the stories depict the massive effort of an American changing the course of destiny through his or her sterling efforts. This is the ultimate American dream. That a truly determined American can change an Angel's actions or God's decision. The arrogance is breathtaking, but it is equally pathetic that such is the ego of the star, director, producer that they seek to outwit God and death.

There's a joke about Doctors, 'What's the difference between God and doctors? Answer: God knows he is not a doctor' Perhaps one could adapt this joke, 'What's the difference between God and Americans, God knows he's not American'. (Disclaimer: I have many American friends who are not at all arrogant so I'm not prejudiced against an entire nation. Just sadly a lot of prominent ones who believe because they can act and are given good scripts, they have ideas that are worth voicing. The ones screened into our living rooms on a daily basis).

As I write a modern travesty appears in the form of Kanye West creating a hologram of Kim Kardashian's late father Robert Kardashian, who famously helped the legal team that saw O J Simpson acquitted of murdering his ex-wife Nicole and her friend Ronald Goldman. Robert Kardashian died of cancer on September 20, 2003. So some 17 years later, what do you give the wife in your life who has riches beyond her dreams and the children she wanted. North and Saint she carried, Chicago and Psalm born by surrogate. There are ways of jumping through hoops when you're that rich and famous. She joked that as she was appearing at The Met Ball, her surrogate had gone in to hospital in labour. Astonishing. So one can sympathise with Kanye's dilemma, as another individual, not only with bipolar phases of mania but also of huge creative talent and rich beyond ones normal dreams. So what do you give to your wife on her 40th that she does not already have or could not have bought herself? He's done the massive wall of roses, the helicopter arrivals, the renting of a basketball stadium just for her and her family for a proposal. By George he came up with a blinder. A hologram of Robert Kardashian which he screened in a private cinema room to close family. Somehow the image appears from the ether and Kanye studied films of Robert Kardashian's body language etc., to create a startling image carrying a message to Kim. He created a speech from heaven. I'm not sure if there is a creative content libel law in California. I imagine there would be and I am quite sure that Robert Kardashian would know all about it. What would he make of this odd piece of theatre? Robert's hologram spoke about how Kim was married to Kanye 'who is the most brilliant genius in the whole world'. Extraordinary time and effort had been taken in presenting this dubious show. Clearly intended as supportive of Kim and her pursuit of passing the bar in California, but still extraordinary in putting words into a dead man's mouth. The family asked friends to leave them privately to watch the hologram repeatedly in private. So they were taken with it. I'm very surprised not one of the siblings didn't storm out in outrage, they normally do. But no they were spellbound by their Dad appearing to them. I suppose Caitlyn Jenner no longer really fulfills the Dad role as she did in the past, so maybe it was timely and another sign of we can be whoever we want to be and we can have whatever we want in life........even if you're dead. It clearly had an effect on them, but what further liberties will rich people take with dealing with death with respect? How can you speak for someone who is dead? The dreaded line jumps to mind, 'it's what he would have wanted?'. Of course it's blindingly obvious we have no clue what he would have wanted and it is no-one's right to claim it.

Hollywood attempts to get that final answer. To go into that world.

I think the first time I really feared hell was when I saw 'What Dreams May Come' with Robin Williams. The demons depicted, the fall into hell before arising was absolutely terrifying. I wondered if the creators of this film were Catholics terrified of hell. In the church of England we tend to mention Heaven a lot more than hell. In fact pretty much everything is tolerated in our church and so long as you say you're sorry you are pretty much OK. We shall look next at religion and the modern religion of Mindfulness, the third wave of Cognitive Behavioural Therapy.

CHAPTER 7

THE THIRD WAVE OF COGNITIVE BEHAVIOURAL THERAPY VERSUS MAINSTREAM RELIGION

So the eastern influence is abundant these days. We here tons of babble about letting go and tons of barely understandable loads of hogwash appear on the internet every day. People I know who I have previously imagined to be reasonably intelligent start posting ridiculous things about Tigers and Monkeys and using some of the elements of these creatures' behaviors in relation to human behavior. We are not monkeys or Tigers. Indeed, if Monkeys or Tigers had enough brain capacity to use Facebook, and read, then they might profit from hearing all sorts of behavioral quirks we humans have that might help them out a lot. Help them to live longer and more productively. No, I will not be tempted by soundbites about Monkeys and bananas, or snakes in the grass or whatever else. If you want to tell me what to do, just do it. Or one can choose a message in the bible. There are plenty of perfectly good parables that Jesus made up about people, that are a lot more relatable and understandable than any amount of animal metaphors.

So maybe this development of the self, so favoured by the third wave of Cognitive Behavioural Therapy (CBT), the Buddhist concepts, is a way of shoring our strength up as individuals so that we can cope with anything.

Even maybe in the face of death. But whilst building up our resilience is of course of great help to those who feel depleted physically and emotionally, there is something very dehumanizing about putting it all onto our own shoulders. Humans need God. The strength of the Cognitive Behavioural Therapeutic movement was that there was science behind it and thus therapy was based around empirically evidenced therapeutic interventions that worked. Once the scene has been clouded with 'Mindfulness' and 'Universal Truths' the science aspect becomes very muddied. Why not just let religion do their thing and therapists do theirs?

In Grayson Perry's 'Rites of Passage' documentary, he follows different approaches to death and mourning. He admits that religion and a need for a God comes out of the ether. It's a great concept. But it is as true an aspect of being human as one can find. For some reason since the beginning of time, wherever you are in the world, you need to have a custom and a shared religious belief system to help you function as a community. It seems to be a survival rite. In the development of the species, humans seem to have fared better by having religion in their lives. For some reason we are currently disabusing ourselves of the notion and turning instead to inner peace, yoga and meditation in its stead. It's a lot of work. A lot of individual work that needs pacing and self-motivation. Established religion, in Boris' words, is kind of 'oven ready'. It has a framework and locations to make it easy to practice. It has set times which are socially adapted. Its community based and family based. Payment is up to the individual, unlike entrance to a theme park, cinema or indeed an expensive yoga studio.

Perry visits a family in Indonesia, who are following the tradition of keeping the corpse of a dead relative in the house for as long as they feel they need to. It is a kind of living grief. They chat around the coffin, asking the advice of the relative on matters of concern in the community or family, as if they are still with them. Apparently the body is somehow embalmed with local herbs, much like the Egyptians did in ancient history, so health concerns are mitigated. Perry sits there with the family around the body and they are talking to and around this body as if they are still very much part of the family. Think the 'Royal Family' with the TV, only one of the characters is dead. The same scene but an embalmed body in the stead of one of the cast. After many months, even a year, finally, the wife, husband or son, decides that they are ready to let go and the funeral is arranged. As a parallel we might see us in our society having a quiet family funeral, followed by a much jollier Memorial Service a year later which everyone can join in with.

It is an interesting way to deal with grief. To keep the person there, even not animated, as a sort of transition and acceptance grows. At a point they are ready to move on without the physical presence of the person.

A friend of mine has a very incapacitated little dog. He's blind, quite deaf, eats very little and only gets out of his little basket in the kitchen to go outside for a pee or a poo. The husband of the couple with Swedish no nonsense, suggested that they could get him stuffed and he could just lie in his basket in the kitchen and carry on the role he has been holding for the last two years. His wife cannot bring herself to say it's enough yet, although she did admit that really it would make no difference really as to the ability for the dog to charm or welcome the family any longer. It reminded me of the staging of the old lady in Grayson Perry's documentary. The placing of the elder in the centre of the room. An inanimate object but with the staging being the same as it had been for years, the absence of the person can gradually be processed without their physical presence being gone. In grief therapy we often ask a child grieving a parent to draw their dining room/kitchen table to show where their Mum or Dad used to sit. The placing of people physically in home settings is very symbolic of the family dynamic and can be highly emotionally charged. How do a family deal with Dad's place at the table when he's gone? Somehow the custom, however bizarre at first, has a kind of logic of coming to terms with the empty space that a death creates. In this way in the Indonesian custom retains the corpse and lets the elder still hold their place in the family and in the community. Whilst now a lifeless body without ability to speak or conjecture, the family still converses around them as if they are still who they were. Perhaps knowing how they would feel about certain issues, there for them to share memories with, albeit a one sided conversation.

In some ways there is also some symbolism here as in the visiting of the grave where the protagonist in a movie or soap or in Ancient Greek theatre or Shakespeare, would talk to the tomb and pour out their reality. Only instead of the slab of stone with writing on it, there is the actual body, embalmed, preserved and still in the home. As bizarre as it sounds there is a sense to it. And when they have done all the talking and they feel that they are ready to move on as a family without that person physically in the house anymore, they 'let go' and have the funeral.

Conversely in our world we are not swayed by a cultural norm in society anymore. There is not really a dominant religion in the UK and if anything we have become our own Gods and priests. Our modern world encourages the development of an ego that exists alone and that as healthy individuals we should be able to control all outside influences by controlling our reaction to it. We are not machines. We are complex thinkers with the capacity to remember our past and fear our future. This is the very essence of the human condition. It's why we are not reckless. It's why we learn from our mistakes, because we remember how painful something was. Of course we do not want to become immobilized by our past or by fear of the future, but this idea that we should only concentrate on the NOW seems highly non-human and very like the brain function of an animal.

It is a natural state for a man to have a God and to have a religion. No animal has a God. This takes away so much stress. If you ask how many people in the UK are religious, no doubt the members of the Church of England have vastly depleted over the last 100 years. However, it only takes a local tragedy to take place for the cameras to be doing a round the clock follow-up at the local church and with the local vicar. The church or synagogue or mosque, even in our modern times is still our touchstone to comfort. What cannot be understood, or forgiven, or tolerated, normally ends up at the church's doorstep. The majesty of the building, the smell of incense, making it in some way otherworldly. Although this of course is a culturally biased notion. Being a member of the Church of England and enjoying bells and smells as they say, there is nothing more reassuring than to walk into a church or a cathedral and smell that majesty. But it only occurred to me when I heard of the Duchess of Sussex (Megan Markle) wanting to put air fresheners around the church in Windsor, that I realized for her being brought up in the US, modern mall like churches are the norm. For her the sense of peace and security would come from such an environment with loud choirs and waving hands up in the air in worship. It makes sense that for her all she smelt was distemper and damp, with mouldy decaying fabric. For me and my compatriots we smell religion. We smell God and organized religion.

Religion gives us a chance to say, 'well I can't make head or tail of this or my grief, can you take it on for me?' Whether you are a natural believer or a humanist or even an atheist; at some time in your life I reckon you will go to church. My mother was a humanist but went to church every week religiously, as they say. She explained to me that the Church of England was a good place to worship being kind and having good morals and helping others before yourself. These Christian principles all conformed to her humanist beliefs. But she did not in reality believe in God. I remember this upsetting me terribly as a rather committed Christian as a little girl and a teenager. I feared she would not be granted eternal peace in heaven unless she changed her ways. I was slightly comforted by Socrates' belief system thinking that she was a very good person and followed moral direction above every other principle. She lived her life giving to others and denying herself so surely by that token she would enjoy life in Heaven. My father went with her to church every week of course as well. He still went long after her death. Dad believed in the faith side as well. Sometimes he was not as 'good' as Mum was, but he believed in God and the spirit and he believed in heaven. For that reason, if there is one, I'm sure they're there together doing 'The Times' crossword whilst sipping sherry.

Bob Geldof rather worryingly expresses his desire for 'suttee' when he dies. He says he does not want to go into a coffin, nor 'a pizza oven'. Suttee is a Hindu practice of immolation. There the husband is burned on a funeral pyre. Bob Geldof imagines it being built with pallets and wood and him being put on there to burn whilst everyone parties around it. I think he sees it as an earthy and freeing ritual. He says he would even convert to Hindu to have it done. However, it also involves the widow sacrificing herself by sitting atop of her husband's funeral pyre. Although it is as such now banned, in rural India it still exists. The idea is that the wife voluntarily throws herself on the pyre. Poor Jeanne Marine. Hope she doesn't feel obliged. Bob could never quite move on could he. Christian missionaries in India were appalled by this practice and thought that women were often forced onto the pyre by relatives who stood to inherit the man's property. So the British made Sati (Suttee) illegal in 1829. References to it and to its abolishment in Nepal at the turn of the twentieth century refer to its abomination and ghastly practice. It is interesting to hear Geldof wax lyrical about it. Is he being sardonic, rebellious, disingenuous? Slightly tongue in cheek and maybe he does not hope that Jeanne Marine jumps onto the pyre, but certainly the freedom and openness is what he seems to want. All these ideas of course of not wanting to be put in a coffin or a pizza oven as he says, are all incumbent on the premise that you are aware of the confines. That in some way you will feel the claustrophobia and be silenced, something Bob Geldof has never liked to be.

Anecdotal Testimony

Fiona had been diagnosed with breast cancer in year 2000. She had 6 rounds of chemotherapy over the next 8 years. She fought each day to stay alive for her boys. She had three sons. One by a first marriage and two by her second marriage which was now dissolved. Her second husband took on looking after the boys, particularly in the latter stages of her illness.

Fiona was a big personality. She was a no-nonsense kind of person, hugely popular and told it how it was. She had a rota of friends who cared for her towards the end of her life. It seemed like the whole community at times were involved. Everyone had watched her hair come and go, which is the outside alert, news headline, the cancer's back. Actually it means someone is having an active attempt to destroy the cancer, but the visual gives away a person's secret. Fiona had tried everything from chemotherapy, caffeine enemas, Swiss retreats, homeopathy, she was desperate to stay alive for her boys.

The last summer she prayed and pleaded to God to just let her have that time with the boys on the beach in the states. Not long after their return she could not hold on any longer. At her death bed she had both her ex- husbands with her. A woman they still loved. She was a powerful presence and she did death her way.

CHAPTER 8

HEAVEN AND HELL

As mentioned, the depiction of hell in 'What Dreams May Come' with Robin Williams was truly terrifying. This film haunted my imagination for a long time after I watched it, because in actual fact it was portrayed in a very convincing and other-worldly way. And I suddenly thought how awful would it be to be a tormented soul. There would be no end to it. It reminds me of my favorite joke.

A man goes to the gates of heaven and is sent down to hell. He meets another bloke there and says, how bad is it here? The other guy says well not too bad at all really. Depends. Do you like greasy food? The bloke says 'yes I love it, but that's what got me, I had a massive coronary attack'. The guy says well on Mondays they serve up Sausages, bacon, baked beans, fried eggs, you name it you can eat all you want. And because you are dead already you can't have a heart attack or feel sick afterwards. Wow the bloke says, that sounds brilliant. The other guy says did you like to drink at all on earth? Well yes the bloke says. Well you will love Tuesdays. They bring in tons of champagne, wine, whisky, beer. You can get as drunk as you like and drink as much as you like. You don't get a hangover because you're dead already. Now did you smoke on earth? Yes sighs the bloke. About 20 a

day.   Well on Wednesday they bring in as many cigarettes as you like, you can just smoke away, no probs. This sounds great says the bloke.   Did you ever do drugs? Asks the guy.   Yes, I'm afraid I did, weed, cocaine, uppers, downers you name it.   Well you'll like Thursdays and Fridays.   They bring in every drug you can think of.   You won't have a bad reaction because you're dead already.   That's amazing says the bloke. Now finally over the weekend, were you a homosexual on earth?   No way says the bloke, straight as you can be.   Oh dear said the other guy, I don't think you are going to like the weekends very much.

So one man's pleasure is another man's poison.   But concepts of heaven and hell seem to me to be more related to a Socratic idea of our own concepts and what we choose to focus on and nurture.   Rather than some generic concept of what hell might look like.   So for me this can easily tie in with Christianity.   That if we live a good life and try to do our best by others and pray for good, then is it not then logical that we might be left in a state of peace at the end of our life.   So that we need to try and get rid of toxic elements in our life.   The Born Again Christians seem to be very focused on the devil. Far more interested on the nasty parts of other people than on the good parts of them.   Judging every situation so as to make some pious point about God.   When actually I never met a mean God in the Church of England.   He was always the nicest, most forgiving, kindest being.   Silly little details of people's sexuality I don't think would bother him in the grand scheme of things, unless someone was being hurt.

The Harry Potter films have some pretty grim depictions of creepy afterlife scenes. These generic depictions are maybe a sum total of what humans would feel they might be afraid of the most. But I find it hard to believe these places actually exist except in our minds. Thus Socrates has always presented to me the most likely concept. That we develop our spiritual side to a point that we may be left in a peaceful state. And if we concentrate on our body too much, then there would be nothing left when we die. Our spiritual being would not be able to survive on, because it had not been developed.

What would be a concept of heaven? I think most people find comfort in the idea of their family and friends being there to greet them. How exactly that would work I cannot imagine. Spiritualists tend to talk vaguely about spirit forces making themselves known with colours or themes. Maybe there would be some encouraging welcoming body that felt comforting to you. Without specifically your Mum or Dad turning up in white robes ready to greet you in heaven. And how would you keep your distance from people who got on your nerves on earth but who had made it up there? Again the idea of Socrates about it being your own personal heaven would make sense. Then the people in your spirit world would be your inclusion, not a celestial's inclusion.

It sounds as if I am contradicting myself. My first criticism of Hollywood is that they try and rewrite the bible and now I seem to be saying that the reality of heaven and hell is entirely personal and within our own minds. What I am actually saying is two things. The first is that we are mere humans and we have a human need for organized religion. We do not cope as well when we are not religious and when we cannot turn to an organized religion for support. I therefore reject overreliance on Third Wave CBT dictates that we should take personal control of all our reactions to everything. So I see a need for religion to hold together people psychologically and to form stable societies. Unfortunately conflicting religious views have often been the cause of hatred and warfare. In fact, this supports the notion that religion and spiritual belief is at the very hub of being human. More important perhaps than food, safety and procreation. There is something about spiritual belief and partaking in rituals that is fundamentally human. It follows therefore that if this belief is threatened by another belief or by another 'clan' that believes in a different religion, then this is ultimately threatening physically and existentially. This is evidence again as to how strong a thing religion is. We dismiss it and its importance at our peril. We need organized religion to support as whilst we are mortal. Whilst we navigate our daily lives, our losses and bad times and our good times.

But if you are asking what actually happens when we die, I find it hard to believe in the traditional ideas of heaven and hell. It makes much more sense to me, as in our dreams, that we make our own afterlife according to the manner in which we have lived our life and how we have developed our soul.

In The Last Days of Socrates, Plato creates the scene of the last days of the Philosopher. Plato (c.429-347 BC) along with Socrates and Aristotle shaped the intellectual tradition of the West for future times. The Socratic questioning technique is as relevant in Psychotherapy today as ever. As a therapist you can help someone make sense of their thinking and problem solving by scaffolding questions in such a way as they gradually find their own answers. Socrates did it like this:

(The Last Days of Socrates, Plato, Penguin Classic)

p.107 *'I want to explain to you how it seems to me natural that a man who has really devoted his life to philosophy should be cheerful in the face of death, and confident of finding the greatest blessing in the next world when his life is finished. I will try to make this clear to you, Simmias and Cebes, how this can be so.*

Ordinary people seem not to realize that those who really apply themselves in the right way to philosophy are directly and of their own accord preparing themselves for dying and death. If this is true, and they have actually been looking forward to death all their lives, it would of course be absurd to be troubled when the thing comes for which they have so long been preparing and looking forward'

Socrates goes on to 'rap' with Simmias asking him a question, leading to a realization from Simmias etc., to promote his thinking on the subject. That philosophers live not for the body but for the soul. That their entire life is spent feeding their soul and not their body. That earthly pleasures are not seen as a growing experience for a philosopher, sex and food and drink. But intellectual pursuits and the acquisition of thinking as the most important quality. If death is the separation of the body from the soul and the soul lives on, then surely a philosopher should not be afraid of death at all.

p113 *'And the desire to free the soul is found chiefly, or rather only, in the true philosopher; in fact the philosopher's occupation consists precisely in the freeing and separation of soul from body. Isn't that so?"*

Cebes says that most men's fear is that the soul will fade shortly after the body goes.

p116 *'But I fancy that it requires no little faith and assurance to believe that the soul exists after death and retains some active force and intelligence'*

Socrates argues that all things are concerned with opposites that come from each other. His argument is that if a body is dead, then the soul is living, the one emerging most strongly from the state of the other.

Socrates further argues that a philosopher who has not indulged his bodily desires but only strengthened his soul through his life has moved close to God within his life and once dead the soul can flow freely into a world with God. Whilst the body indulged throughout life, with the needs of the flesh, p.134 *'....they are compelled to wander about these places as a punishment for their bad conduct in the past'*

So the concepts of Heaven and Hell (Hades) are laid out. This philosophical concept that every religion adopts as their model. But in structured religions all the rules are laid out and praying for forgiveness is an option for redemption. However, the philosopher sees it as driven by the self. This idea is perhaps the start of the ego driven movement.

In psychotherapy using the Cognitive approach to therapy, the client is encouraged to challenge their own versions of truth, or what they tell themselves everyday, in other words 'their internal voice'.

'Once patients are more reliably able to identify their painful automatic thoughts, the process of answering

back to these thoughts (or putting them on trial) can begin. This is the phase of therapy in which Socratic dialogue becomes critical. Socratic dialogue, a series of interconnected questions to reach a more logical, objective conclusion about one's inner experiences, is a common theme for all cognitive techniques. In fact, asking open-ended and open-minded questions is probably one of the most critical and distinguishing features of CBT. Four basic steps in the questioning process have been described: (1) characterizing the problem specifically and accurately; (2) identifying the associated thoughts, beliefs, and interpretations: (3) understanding the meanings of the thoughts for the patient; and (4) assessing the consequences of thoughts and their basis in evidence. Socratic questions should neither lead not trap the patient into agreeing with the therapist's view (which of course if inevitably biased) and are intended to stimulate consideration of alternative perspectives and uncover information that was not previously considered'.

(p.8 Cognitive-behavioral Therapy with Adults, A guide to Empirically-informed Assessment and Intervented. Edited by Stefan G Hoffmann and Mark A Reinecke Cambridge University Press 2010)

Socrates did bend the listener in the direction of his thoughts, guided them to enlightenment through skilled questions which helped the pupil find their truth. In CBT the practitioner must be careful not to prepare scaffolded questioning to attain a truth that sits nicely with some theory they may personally hold about the root of the client's problem. But the 'forensic' as we sometimes refer to this questioning technique is to challenge the previously held explanations that the client has established. The client may have had a belief reinforced through their upbringing, their school, their friendship group and by the evidence they provide to future friends or work colleagues. People tend to accept what someone else tells them about themselves. In CBT the Socratic approach challenges preconceived notions and truths and asks for evidence to support the belief. Frequently the client cannot support the tightly held belief system with evidence. Frequently they find abundant support to challenge their belief system. The more their old story is deconstructed with facts and evidence, the more the client can build a new narrative that actually fits the evidence and the truth.

The CBT movement moves away from the Freudian theories of familial patterns that are deterministic. Deterministic in that they can never be changed, or only after total dissembling and rebuilding of the psyche with the analyst as the mother figure. CBT is a technique that allows the client more 'agency' in their own recovery. They work out how to challenge themselves and how to present themselves in a different light with a different narrative so that all their relationships change as a byproduct of the changed narrative.

Anecdotal Testimony

Penelope had been in some denial about her father's illness. He had a brain tumour and despite operations and chemotherapy, nothing was working. Her father had been a fun character and they had lived in Hong Kong, loving the ex- pat life and their household resounded with activity and laughter. When her father was diagnosed with a brain tumour all that life stopped. Suddenly his work had to post him back to the UK so his medical care would be taken care of there. His whole family clearly had to move with him. So his illness meant that Penelope's life was turned upside down. Aged 13 she left everything she had ever known and loved. Her school, her friends, her fun life in Hong Kong. They moved to Ipswich and Penelope went to a school she hated. She felt like an outsider. She was an outsider. She felt very resentful that her Dad had got ill and now because of that their whole life had changed. Plus, he wasn't fun anymore. He didn't have a laugh. His personality changed. He was grumpy and monosyllabic. Penelope hated it so much that she dreaded going into to his room to see him.

Penelope needed a break her Mum thought. To take a trip to France and meet up with a family they knew from Hong Kong. That would put the smile back on her face. When she arrived home it was clear that she had had a ball. Go upstairs and tell Dad all about it, her Mum suggested. I will tomorrow Penelope promised. She didn't want today to be spoilt by seeing him. That night he had his final seizure and died. Penelope lived with guilt about how she had dealt with her father's death. So much so that she didn't even tell her school friends that he had died. She just never had them over so she could keep her secret.

CHAPTER 9

THE SOUL

There has been research in science historically and examples of the distinction between the point where death replaces life. Where the internal driving, beating being, ceases beating, driving and stops. And whilst it can be scientifically argued that the matter almost instantly takes on chemical changes and parasitical activity starts thriving in the body, the internal axis of the human has stopped and now the life and organic and chemical activity is a post mortem activity, not a living activity actioned by the human's biological make up. It is at this point that many religions argue that the soul leaves the body.

The concept of a soul and the pictorial imagery adorns many religious works of art throughout the ages and in primitive drawings. It has been a consistent theme/concept almost from the birth of time. It is particularly human this idea that the moment a body becomes just that, the soul has parted.

In Ancient Greek soul or psyche translates 'to breathe' but incorporating in that meaning. The breathing, the soul includes reason, character, feeling, consciousness, memory, perception, thinking etc. To all intents and purposes that would mean in a scientific sense, all cognitive functions driven by the brain. We know in psychological terms our personality is mainly dictated by our frontal lobal brain and our amygdala. Anyone who has the misfortune of having a relative or friend who sustains serious or even mild frontal lobal injury can see there can be a quite serious change in their personality, not only attributable to psychological trauma.

James Cracknell and his wife Beverley Turner split up after a nine-year struggle following his frontal lobal brain injury. In 2010 Cracknell was hit by a lorry's wing mirror during a cycle ride across the United States. The damage slowed his speech and left him with a terrible temper. During an interview with The Telegraph in 2012, a neuropsychologist told them as they left hospital that 75% of people where one of the couple has a brain injury end in divorce. In that interview they were trying desperately to be the 25% with Beverley joking that 'We're not allowed to divorce'.

Beverley also said that she 'missed him'. In referring to missing him she is talking about the him that she knew before brain injury. Which strongly implies that it is not just death that takes the 'soul' away if the 'soul' is your personality. She missed that quintessential part of him that made him James, her husband. He had become someone else. She describes having to be quite firm with him, treating him almost like a child for his own good. Clearly this was not what she had signed up for. Nor he, because the bit of him that still loved challenges was very much there. Hence he decided to go off to University to study an MPhil, even though he was married with children and had responsibilities at home.

Another example is with patients presenting with Alzheimer's and dementia who frequently display behavioural symptoms such as moodiness, apathy, changes in personality, unsocial behaviours and language difficulty.

The Well Institute for Neurosciences at the Memory and Aging Center finds that people with dementia often act in ways that are very different from their 'old self' and it is those changes that are hard for family and friends to deal with. The scientific explanation is that the person is losing neurons (cells) in parts of the brain. The 'behavior changes' you see often depend on which part of the brain is losing cells. The Frontal Lobe deals with thinking, memory, behavior and movement. Parietal Lobe deals with language and touch. Occipital Lobe deals with vision. The Cerebellum with balance and coordination. The Temporal Lobe deals with hearing, learning and feelings. The Brain Stem regulates breathing, heart rate and temperature.

The reason as to why Frontal Lobe damage causes such devastating effects on personality is that it controls our ability to focus, pay attention and be motivated. When cells in the frontal lobe are lost people are less able to plan and stay focused. They are often less motivated and become passive. The frontal lobes also control our impulses. Someone with frontal lobe damage people may behave rudely or insensitively.

With Alzheimer's a person may become forgetful and struggle to follow conversations, getting distressed and angry because the noise is overstimulating.

Interestingly they may, much like a baby or toddler, become reliant on emotional cues and start becoming anxious or worried if their caregiver is feeling that way.
A lack of ability to communicate pain or what they are feeling may also be indicated by acting out or with anger. Urinary tract infections, constipation and poor sleep are examples of conditions that can cause sudden and dramatic behavioural changes.

One very key distressing element for a family member is seeing a much admired figure in the family lose their sense of propriety, appropriateness and manners. The order of behavior that rates us in our society and distinguishes us from animals. When inappropriate behavior becomes the norm, shame is felt and the family member can become consumed in their attempts to cover up the behavior. A humorous example of this in popular culture is Hyacinth Bucket and her 'Daddy'. The story lines imply that her father is running around naked and molesting women. Hyacinth goes to great lengths to either be in denial, or explain away how hot

Daddy gets or how kind Daddy is etc., to avoid the glaring obvious issue that the rest of her family is facing. Most caregivers kindly reprimand or remind the patient that is not what we do, remember we do this or that, just like we would do with a small child.

There is a difference then surely between death and the soul departing, if the soul is defined as a combination of cognitive attributes and 'personality', that part of the brain that makes us who we are. The study of changes in personality and behavior suggests that our soul changes as bits of neurons die off. So a partial death of the soul?

The soul once it leaves the body, according to which religion or belief system you adhere to, goes into immortality, another place etc. Following the logic above about the soul being the living aspects of your brain making you a particular individual, then partial death of the brain would be hard to explain in terms of where those dead bits of your soul go to?

In Judaism and in Christianity the belief is we have a soul 'anima' but only humans are immortal. In Hinduism and Jainism the belief is that all living thigs are souls (Atman, jiva) and have their physical representation in the world. Some believe even objects such as mountains have souls, this is called 'animism'.

Anima, referring to life is rather terrifyingly referred to in hospitals in France. The Reanimation room is where they bring you back as it were after an operation. Well clearly it would be more terrifying not to reanimated, but there it as used not as in recovery in English, but having been under general anesthetic with respiratory machines taking over the function as your brain cannot instruct your lungs to open and close whilst under anesthesia, then they have to give you other drugs to 'reanimate' you.

In English we used the word 'soul' from the Old English 'sawol, sawel' first seen in the 8th century poem Beowulf. The Germanic route and Nordic route giving 'seula, sela' respectively. The Germanic route of this word is believed to come from 'coming from or belonging to the sea (or lake)' because of the Germanic and pre-Celtic belief that souls emerge from and return to sacred lakes or sea.

In Ancient Egyptian religion a human was believed to be made up of both physical and spiritual elements. In Babylonia, an 8th century Royal official from Sam'al ordered a stele (a huge finger shaped black stone where rules are carved on) to be erected on his death. The inscription asked that mourners celebrate his life and afterlife with feasts 'for my soul that is in this stele'. It is an extraordinary aspect of our humanity that from whence archaeologists have been in a position to uncover such pieces of incredible history (uncovered by

Neubauer Expedition of the Oriental Institute of Chicago, Illinois), that such a mainstream thought is still so central to our idea of life and death. A mortal body, buried with commemoration and respect for the life in some form of service or celebration and a belief that the soul will enjoy an afterlife. Even with aforementioned scientific deconstruction of the brain and which parts of the brain affect which bits of our body and our personality and behavior, we are still today just as conversant with a concept of our souls. Because there is still some part of us that believes that we are more individual than the sum parts of our brain anatomy, our behaviours and experience.

The Bahai Faith says that *'the soul is a sign of God, a heavenly gem whose realty the most learned of men hath failed to grasp, and whose mystery no mind, however acute, can ever hope to unravel' (Bhahullah, 1976, Gleanings from the Writings of Bahaullah, Wilmette, Illinois:Bahai Publishing Trust. Pp 158-63)*

Bahaullah stated that the soul continues to live after the physical death of the human body and is immortal. Heaven can be seen as a state of nearness to God and hell as a state of remoteness from God. Each state is in respect to the individual's efforts to develop spirituality. Bahaullah taught that individuals have no experience prior to their life on earth and the soul's evolution is always towards God and away from the material world. In this faith there is much of Plato's thinking. We are on earth to develop our spirituality and to rely less and less on our physicality and our physical possessions.

Buddhism has many branches but in universal terms there is an idea that everything is in a state of flux and that humans are also in flux and has no permanent self. Accordingly, there is 'no-self' or 'no soul'. This is the *anatta* doctrine. The translation of 'no soul' is complex as if soul is described as something everywhere and in everything that continues after death, then there is not a rebuttal of the concept of a soul, but just that it denies that there is a permanent entity that remains constant behind all the changing bodily parts of a human being. The belief is that mental states come up and die with no 'thinker' behind them. After the body dies these mental processes continue and are reborn in a new body. Because of the constant state of flux and process these new mental processes are neither the same as before nor totally different.

In Tibetan Buddhism there are three minds: very subtle mind (which lives on after death), subtle mind (dies with the physical, this is the 'dreaming mind' and gross mind which does not exist when sleeping (which also perishes with death). Very subtle mind does carry on and when it 'catches on' or coincides with phenomena again, a new subtle mind emerges with its own personality/assumptions/habits, and that entity experiences karma in the current continuum.

There are Buddhists who prefer an agnostic position re rebirth or reincarnation. Other Buddhists point to research where evidence has been established at the University of Virginia, suggesting that some people are reborn.

The Buddhist description of different minds as above, the very subtle mind, the subtle mind and the gross mind seem to tally with descriptions of neuroscience looking at the activity of different levels of consciousness. Using brain imaging it is possible to see what part of the brain is activated when thinking and using cognitive processes such as talking, reading and doing Mathematics. Other activity becomes highlighted when sleeping and that in itself is not one dimensional, as described in the concept of a 'subtle mind'. There are different parts of the brain activity involved in shallow sleep, in deep REM sleep. It seems a simplistic concept, which is readily relatable, but not scientifically provable. And the 'very subtle mind' being the one that many would associate with other religions/belief systems as being the soul, the anima, the essence of a person. Where does that show up on a scan? Why do I persist in attempting to prove a soul is there using scientific principles? Because historically everything that has ever come down to mystery, usually ends up being evidenced scientifically. Why should the soul be any different? Where is the soul?

The current scientific consensus is that there is no evidence to support the existence of any kind of soul.

Julien Musolino believes that the human mind is like a complex machine that operates with the same physical laws as any and all other objects in the universe. He says:

'there is currently no scientific evidence whatsoever to support the existence of the soul… there is also considerable evidence that seems to indicate that souls do not exist'

(Musolino, Julien, 2015, The Soul Fallacy: What Science Shows We Gain from Letting Go of Our Soul Beliefs. Amherst, New York: Prometheus Books pp. 21-38)

But the search for the soul has been an important part of advancing the study of the human body to really understand that significant difference that makes us human and individual. There have been two contrasting dominant concepts in Scientific exploration, one seeing the soul as spiritual and immortal and the other seeing it to be material and mortal.

Neuroscience, particularly cognitive neuroscience operates under the ontological assumption of physicalism. So that any action must be described and explained in physical terms. That mental phenomena is entirely physical and that human thought and behavior is caused entirely by physical processes in the brain. To evidence these explanations functional neuroimaging is used to study various cognitive processes. The evidence shows that all processes of the mind have physical correlates in brain function. However, imaging cannot explain whether neural activity plays a causal role in the occurrence of these cognitive processes.

Identification of causation and of necessary and sufficient conditions requires explicit experimental manipulation of that activity. If manipulation of brain activity changes consciousness, then a causal role for that brain activity can be inferred.

(Farah, Martha J, Murphy, Nancey, 2009, "Neuroscience and the Soul". Science 323 (5918): 1168 https://pubmed.ncbi.nlm.nih.gov/19251609)

Two common types of manipulation experiments are loss of function and gain of function experiments. In the loss example a part of the nervous system is diminished or removed to see if it is necessary (necessity) for a certain process to occur. In the other gain condition (sufficiency) an aspect of the nervous system is increased. This type of experiment can be achieved using direct electrical brain stimulation, magnetic brain stimulation using transcranial magnetic stimulation, psycho-pharmalogical manipulation, optogenetic manipulation and through study of brain damage through case studies.

Physics can tease at the concept of a dramatic new theoretical explanatory framework with particles not explored or discovered in previous experiments. Some theorists have invoked quantum indeterminism as a possible explanatory mechanism for soul/brain interaction. But this has been debunked by neuroscientists who have found no evidence that such processes play a role in brain function. Peter Clark (neuroscientist) concluded that a Cartesian soul has no basis from quantum physics.

(Clark, Peter, 2014 Neuroscience, Quantum Indeterminism and the Cartesian Soul, https://www.ncbi.nlm.nih.gov.pubmed.24355546)

The Cartesian soul is named in honour of Descartes. The central claim is that of dualism, the immaterial mind and the material body whilst being ontologically distinct substances, causally interact. This idea continues in many non-European philosophies).

The difficulty still persists then that we cannot seem to locate this soul of ours. We can sort of feel it, or we think we can, but where is it? The philosophical neurosurgeon soon encounters difficulties when localizing the abstract concepts of mind and soul within the tangible 1300-gram organ with 100 billion neurons. Gradually over the years through accident and pursuit neuroscientists and neurosurgeons have found their way roughly around the brain, oh that bit that does and that bit acts on another bit that does that. The functional magnetic resonance studies tells us a lot more about the extensive network of neurons in the cerebral hemispheres.

The neurosurgeons found their way to deeper areas of the brain the brain stem has been found to be particularly delicate and vulnerable. We know that when there is brain death after irreversible damage to it, it is clear that the brainstem is essential for life, because it is through this that all the messages sent to the body are conducted through. Theoretically this might be a good explanatory framework for the place where the soul is situated. Not in the heart (we can replace that with a pig's heart or another person's heart), nor in the lungs, but the brainstem might be a more logical place for such an essence to exist.

Neurologists and neurosurgeons are ranked high amongst scientists involved in the philosophical debate concerning what might extend beyond the physical world. The reason being is that they are constantly involved with patients who have fallen into unconsciousness.

'In their attempts at restoring normalcy to bodies and minds, they also grapple with life and death. Inevitably, they ponder spirituality and the dominion of the soul'

(Understanding Brain, Mind and Soul: Contributions from Neurology and Neurosurgery Sunil K Pandya MS Neurosurgeon, Jaslok Hospital & Research Centre, Dr G

V Deshmukh Marg. Mumbai Mens Sana Monogr. 2011 Jan-Dec; 9(1) 129-149)

In electro stimulatory operations on epileptic patients that memories might be evoked, Neurosurgeons have discovered an extraordinary capacity of the brain, that wrapped up in the brain are memories that the patient can recall the scenario within that memory and the emotion felt at the time. Similar phenomena occur in hypnosis, rebirthing procedures, repressed memories (although there is some debate still about the reliability of repressed memories).

The imaging techniques can show up emotions as has been mentioned. It can show the brain being lit up more for example when someone has experienced deep grief and words associated with grief related words and neutral words.

'Nucleus accumbens activity in response to grief-related vs neutral words that was significantly greater in the complicated grief group compared to the non-complicated grief group' (O'Connor et al., 2008)

But the central questions of the location or existence of a soul is still not answered by these findings. We know that a person's brain will light up (i.e. react more) if they have been sensitized emotionally with grief. So their brain make-up and how they respond to the outside input (in this case hearing words that either are triggering or neutral) will be different according to their recent or perhaps not so recent life experience. So the brain is not a static entity and neither are all the connections that it is made up of. It is an extraordinary complicated set of hormones, sensory connections, but essentially it functions with complex linkages with internal and external drivers. But this is still describing the mind, an individual's mind, on a certain day, after a certain experience, before or after an injury. That is their mind. Changing and evolving due to billions of connections, the external life experiences, the medications being taken, the drugs that have been used or abused. It is not static. But we are still not talking about the concept of the soul, or where it is?

The soul is perhaps considered as an essence, an intangible quality that is within us. It is more than a description of someone's personality when we conjecture on the nature of the soul. There are always it seems more questions than answers. Anton Chekhov, who was originally a physician, wrote to his friend Suvorin (7 May, 1889) and said,

'I think that when dissecting a corpse, the most inveterate spiritualist will be bound to ask himself, Where is the soul here? And if one knows how great is the likeness between bodily and mental diseases, and that both are treated by the same remedies, one cannot help refusing to separate the soul from the body'

Leonardo da Vinci placed the soul above the optic chiasm in the region of the anterior-inferior third ventricle. He lived in 1452-1519. Extraordinary that in some senses he was as near to an explanation as we are today.

In 1907 Dr Duncan MacDougall of Haverhill, Massachusetts devised an experiment in which he would weigh a person as they died and thus work out the weight of the soul. So in believing that clearly the soul must weigh something and that believing that at the moment of death the soul leaves the body, there should be the desired weight loss at that moment.

'My first subject was a man dying of tuberculosis. It seemed to me best to select a patient dying with a disease that produces great exhaustion, the death occurring with little or no muscular movement, because in such a case the beam could be kept more perfectly at balance and any loss occurring readily noted.' 'The patient was under observation for three hours and forty minutes before death, lying on a bed arranged on a light framework built upon very delicately balanced platform beam scales. The patient's comfort was looked after in every way, although he was practically moribund when placed upon the bed. He lost weight slowly at the rate of one ounce per hour due to evaporation of moisture in respiration and evaporation of sweat. During all three hours and forty minutes I kept the beam end slightly above balance near the upper limiting bar in order to

make the test more decisive if it should come. At the end of three hours and forty minutes he expired and suddenly coincident with death the beam end dropped with an audible stroke hitting against the lower limiting bar and remaining there with no rebound. The loss was ascertained to be three-fourths of an ounce'.

This experiment was repeated with 5 other patients (struggle to say participants) used in the experiments. He concluded thus that the soul weighs 0.5 to 1.5 ounces (Mac Dougall, 1907)

It is hard not to think what nonsense. I mean it's a valid attempt to locate that mysterious thing that is the soul. Well, guess it must weigh something. But as always this searching for that immortal essence that we call the soul, is it not just the human desire for there to be more? It is so hard to see any logical explanation for it being a physical thing in our body that travels out. And yet it's 'existence' as a concept is universal. If you are human you are probably going to at some stage consider your soul and whether it's going to live on after you are physically dead. And if you have lost a person close to you, you are going to wonder if their soul is around, or content, or unhappy. There will no doubt be times when you hope that there is no immortal soul. You hear of people berating the actions of someone in the family and saying, 'your grandfather would be turning in his grave'. So at the same time acknowledging the immortal nature of how we know what people who were close to us believed and thought was right and wrong, but also that they at least are not here to witness the dreadful behavior. It is how we keep our relatives and friends alive.

My cousin recently asked how our deceased father would have voted, or what he would have thought about Brexit. He was a historian and pragmatist rather than passionate about politics. He viewed politics, as most historians do I imagine, as an observer and predictor of what will happen or might happen based on the examples in history. My eldest sister said she wasn't sure, she would think about it. We then all agreed that he would never have agreed with there being a referendum in the first place. That is not to say we would know whether he would be pro leaving the EU, or remaining within it, but he would have strongly believed that it was the duty of the politicians to make those sensible decisions, not to let the public have a say. And then I remembered all the times that he would talk about the idiocy of referendums and almost a desertion of responsibility when politicians turn to them. He used to cite that the common man would almost certainly vote for the re-introduction of the death penalty should they be offered the chance. I am not sure if that would be the same now in our woke society, but in the 70s when he was pontificating on the subject it was the case. He argued that the death penalty was barbaric and in a civilized country we do not kill bad people.

So whilst discussing the rights and wrongs of the whole Brexit debacle, Dad was part of the discussion. Posthumously. We remembered what he said whilst he was alive and so we could fairly confidently turn to him for his wisdom years after his death and even more years since his wisdom had unfortunately for the most part deserted him through vascular dementia. The essence of our fully cognitively functioning Dad was still there. Is still there.

It is on a daily basis that the dead in my life are thought about. My Mum, my Dad. They are there as I talk to my family, friends and adult children. Not with a tragic voice, because to be fair they were both old and as a family we don't do dramatizing of death. Remember the good and the bad and have a laugh about it. Even with my more scientific and logical brain than a superstitious brain, I sometimes hope Mum cannot hear me slagging her off for her negligence. I think how much it would upset her and I wouldn't want to upset her or hurt her feelings. Completely illogical nonsense. But then I am human and we really cannot be sure it's just our superstition and our human way of coping with grief and fear.

V.S. Ramachandran a brain scientist at the University of San Diego is rather blunt and said in an interview:

'there might be soul in the sense of the universal spirit of the cosmos, but the soul as it is usually spoken of, 'an

immaterial spirit that occupies individual brains and that only evolved in humans – all that is complete nonsense'

He viewed the belief in the soul as superstition.

Whilst scientists who have faith see their faith and the soul as an intangible. Very much how belief is described. You either have it or you don't. You have been touched by the spirit or you haven't. So to look for the soul as a material thing in a scientific search is illogical in its essence. It is already a faulty logic. Dr Kenneth R Miller at Brown University would say to students or other academics:

'As a scientist, I have nothing to say about the soul. It's not a scientific idea' (Dean, 2007)

CHAPTER 10

PARANORMAL ACTIVITY

So is there any evidence to persuade us that there is life after death? More than in the sense that has just been alluded to where we remember the views and beliefs and quirks of our deceased. We remember the perfume they wore, their favorite colour. But is there evidence to suggest that indeed they are alive in another universe, or still with us in spirit?

The human heart has an amazing ability to see some meaning wherever they look. Despite science repeatedly failing to find any validity in mediums or psychics. Humans have a need for religion, for an afterlife and for a relevance that appeals to their narcissistic needs.

I am reminded of a joke that Peter Kay tells about a funeral for Connie and everyone discussing it:

'Did you see it was pissing with rain, but as coffin was lowered the clouds parted and the bloody sun shone. That were Connie that did that. That were Connie. I said No that was the weather. No, no that were Connie weren't it Lina. Lina says 5 years ago I lost my Billy he loved Cheese and Onion crisps, he loved Quavers. Couldn't move for Quavers in our house. Multipacks. And when they lowered the coffin into the ground, I

swear on our Christine's eyes, God as my witness, an empty bag of Quavers blew across graveyard, that were Billy, he were there'.

In psychological terms it is described as confirmation bias or myside bias. In other words, our brains may have seen lots of Quavers bags on the ground, but if we are feeling strongly about someone, we will be much more receptive in acknowledging and feeling the meaning of something we see. So if someone believes in the afterlife and that a spirit will send them a message, they will look very hard to have that belief acknowledged. People display this bias when they gather or remember information selectively, or when they interpret something in a biased way. This bias becomes even more entrenched when emotionally charged issues or beliefs are at stake. Belief perseverance is when despite someone having their belief proved to be false, that the person holds on to the belief still. *(Baron, Jonathan, 2000, Thinking and deciding (3rd edition) New York: Cambridge University Press)*

I might put Homeopathy in this category. Despite repeated trials proving Homeopathy does not work clinically, it has devoted followers. A client of mine whose child had had repeated ear infections, which finally resulted in the eardrum bursting, had been treated repeatedly with homeopathy. Finally, the Doctor insisted the child be given antibiotics and that the parents actually make sure the child takes them. The child's ear recovered. The client said, well the homeopathy finally worked.

Lady Glenconner was a lady in waiting to Princess Margaret and has recently penned her autobiography/memoir entitled 'A Lady in Waiting: My Extraordinary Life in the Shadow of the Crown' She says that her inspiration was due to being asked so much about her life and how things worked with the crown to help with the latest series of 'The Crown' on Netflix. During this time she realized that she had quite a few stories to tell and that people were interested in them. Apart from a vast array of eccentricity and humour there are very dark places in her life. Two of her sons died. One son had a terrible bike accident on a gap year and ended up in a coma for months where she had all but lost hope of his recovery.

When her son Henry died of Aids she was devastated that she had just missed his death. She had been arriving at the hospital, as usual, and a nurse said that he had died. Lady Glenconner struggled with the grief and felt at a loss. Her son had turned to Buddhism and it had become a central part of his life.

"My close friend Margaret Vyner understood I needed support and knowing how devoted Henry was to Buddhism, she took me out to India to stay with Mitch Crites, our mutual friend who had got Colin out of

trouble when he'd started a fight with an Indian shopkeeper several years before. I was absolutely exhausted and didn't want to go but Mitch reassured me, telling me how healing India was. He told me, 'Death is a part of daily life and it isn't uncommon to see a body being cremated on a funeral pyre flating off on the river. The culture embraces death: they talk about and they see it.'"

This theme of seeing it regularly and dealing with it, without euphemisms seems at the crux of where we have dehumanized death in some way. We have tried to pretend it isn't what it is. We have tried to detach ourselves from its reality, even in the words such as 'she's passed', or 'crossed the rainbow bridge' or any way of avoiding the reality of death. This is not to say that we need to distance ourselves from religion and ritual. This has always been a human way of dealing with what we cannot deal with by ourselves. Religion is a structural need for humans, even now. The fact that Henry turned to Buddhism when he had Aids was almost certainly because he needed a ritual to help him cope. Whilst he was suffering in hospital Lady Glenconner said there would be lots of Buddhists chanting with him which gave him great comfort.

"I was so grateful to Margaret and Mitch because as soon as I arrived I knew it was the right decision – everything Mitch had said was true, and I felt a sense of relief straight away. They took me along to different

temples: to Jain temples, which looked like they'd been made out of lace, and we watched the monks in devotion, wearing nothing but a feather fan over their groins. The nuns wore white garments, their bodies bundled up, so they looked like huge white meringues.

We went into one of these temples and found a family mourning a family member who had died, in the middle of a puja, a Hindu form of worship. They were bunched together, clapping and chanting, moving in a rhythmic unison. Mitch went up to them and said, 'I've got a lady with me whose son has just died. He was a Buddhist. Do you mind if she watches you?'

'No, no, she can't watch, she must join in!' they said, opening their arms to me. I felt a huge sense of release when I was swept up in their puja, as they burned incense and chanted.

We carried on visiting more temples but I started to get worried: in Buddhism, it is believed that when the deceased has reached a certain level in their journey to nirvana there has to be a Buddhist monk chanting a prayer at the precise time of this journey to help the person reach the next level. The process is the same for everyone and therefore, on a set day and time, a few weeks after the death, this prayer has to happen.

On that particular day, we were driving and hadn't found anywhere with monks to chant the prayer. I knew the time slot was a slim one, so I began to get anxious on behalf of Henry. We were in the middle of nowhere, driving down a long road in the desert, when Mitch said to me, 'Don't worry. I am absolutely certain we will find a monk'.

I didn't know why Mitch was so sure, since there was nothing but camels and palm trees, but then we saw a lone figure on the road. Mitch said, 'I think this is what we've been waiting for,' and stopped the car.

Mitch, who spoke Hindi, explained and the monk smiled and took my hands at once, starting the puja for Henry. I couldn't help but feel it was a sign that this monk, the only person we had passed on the whole journey, was there for me, for Henry, and that Henry was all right. He was at peace."

This extract from Lady Glenconner's book, whilst long, seemed too important to precis. Because it sums up beautifully the need to grieve and to find symbolism. Somehow back in stuffy London, grieving over a young man with Aids was a tough ask. It would become all about the illness and not about missing her son and hoping he was now OK. So her good friend understood that a pilgrimage was what she needed. And being who she is, she was taken on one and all the right things happened in the right order. Part of grief therapy recognizes stages of grieving, but it is common for people to get stuck. They become rooted in grief and somehow cannot move past it. It not only affects them but those they love around them. A young death particularly has a sort of contagion. There is the death and then the emotional ripples from that death.

Lady Glenconner found meaning in the monk being there against all the odds. For her it felt like a sign. Serendipity, looking for something and finding just what you needed. Horace Walpole, a member of the House of Commons in the 18th century found he had a talent for finding just what he needed when he needed it. With serendipity the idea is that it's not just enough to imagine what you need you have to move. The human capacity to find our way to places where there are people, ideas, or things that provide us with what we have been seeking.

Jung created two definitions around synchronicity. One is the intense emotion produced in the coincider. Jung called this numinous (intensely religious, spiritual, divine). Some Jungians define synchronicity by its pragmatic effect. A meaningful coincidence must assist in psychological change – individuation. From these early definitions there has evolved a wider definition that Synchronicity is an intentional message from the universe.

The fact that Lady Glenconner got such meaning from finding this monk at the right time gave her enormous comfort. For her it was a sign. We need signs to comfort us and possibly when we are most distressed we are on the lookout to find them.

We are somehow hardwired to look for signs and symbols. From an evolutionary standpoint it makes little sense, except at the higher spectrum of human functioning. If evolutionary success is achieved through being sensitive to noises, smells, sounds that might be dangerous and responding quickly and evasively, then through natural selection those with a more developed amygdala would be the survivors. And as these survivors passed on their genes successfully to the following generations, the natural selection of those humans with larger amygdalas would be the result. In today's world there is ample evidence that our natural fear and flight mechanism is very much in evidence and a lot of research and therapeutic skills are applied in efforts to attempt to switch this control off. Because of course now our stress comes in business meetings, or stuck on the tube or whatever, and fleeing is either impossible, embarrassing and in any event not lifesaving.

So we are stuck it seems with this annoying primitive survival mechanism. But why did we develop intuition or sensitivity to symbolism and meaning when there is no meaning? Could it be that we survived more efficiently if we coped with tragedy through finding a way for our higher mind to be soothed by a symbol or belief system? Could it be that natural selection favored those who were pragmatic with grief and looked to find meanings to soothe their 'souls'. Souls are referred to herein inverted commas because they are not a physical entity in a human being, souls are constructed artifices to refer to some part of the mind that we do not have a physical evidence of. So if one took as a hypothetical concept that people survived better if they had a brain that looked for symbols or signs, how would that work in terms of natural selection? It is possible that young men would be less reckless in hunting, or in their behavior if they had a meaning to live by. That an elder in a community might push through and not give up if they had a place in the community of meaning. It would make sense that a community built with symbols and meanings would be healthier psychologically, if not physically more likely to survive and reproduce. With a nod to structuralism, this survival mechanism reaches much further than just physical and mental attributes to survival. It reaches out to another dimension, one of unscientific ideas but that can be scientifically proved to be effective. A bit like the placebo effect. We can scientifically evidence that giving a sugar pill can persuade a proportion of people to feel better in certain circumstances, sometimes as much as the evidenced medicine. So science has already experimented with nonsense with humans and found it can be effective. So if a person believes a feather found on the ground is evidence that their mother is watching them from heaven, so they better behave and do good by their kids or their family or community, this can have a profound effect on behavior. If the person did not believe the feather signified anything other than that a bird had lost a feather there, then there might be no incentive to behave well or to reflect on the values of their mother and what she had taught them growing up etc. Certainly if there is no belief system of any sort it is more challenging to be bothered to live well it seems.

But we all know someone who fervently believes in oblique messages from dead relatives. A person who has a psychic ability. And despite my scientific head strongly denying such a possibility I would say that I am touched by this gift myself. I interpret it differently however. So when my Mother died I had moments when I felt a touch on my back. A very physical touch, like a hug. Another time the phone rang and I picked it up and there was no one on the other end. I did 1471, which I think I remember correctly was the old number in the UK on a landline you could ring to see what the number was that had rung you last. And I nearly was sick when the number recalled was the phone number from my childhood home 'The Haven' on Harrow-on-the-Hill. I was absolutely shocked. I don't think anyone believed me except for a very good friend who considered herself an expert at seeing dead people. She said that my Mother was reassuring me that she was alright and not to be so sad, that she was there comforting me.

My Mother also used to say that a robin appearing was the sign of someone you love saying hello. And every Christmas Day I see a robin in the garden. Mum, always not wanting to make a fuss and inevitably creating a big one, obligingly died on Christmas morning. So there she is every Christmas morning saying hi to me. Robins are traditionally associated with Christmas with some saying that robins arrived in the stable soon after Jesus was born and whilst Joseph gathered wood for the fire, they used their wings like bellows to keep the embers alight. The Virgin Mary gave them their fiery red breast in thanks.

So of course Christmas is a great time to see robins as all the other birds have gone somewhere warmer. And robin's redbreasts stand out in the winter garden. But my confirmation bias is at work. My mother and I shared this sort of psychic link. Despite not being close emotionally there was this extraordinary 6th sense between us. I had a near death experience in France during the bastille celebrations in Normandy. I had gone for a holiday there with my boyfriend (future husband) and discovered there that I had a terrible allergy to sulphites in red wine. We had bought a cheapest of cheap bottle of red wine, rammed full of sulphites and had drunk it whilst playing Trivial Pursuit in our gite. I went to bed finding it extremely difficult to breathe. I felt faint and my chest was wheezing and I had an extremely disturbed night during which a soldier appeared with a red military uniform and brass buttons by my bedside and beckoned me to go with him. I resisted leaving. But I felt totally terrified and immobile. The next day I could not shake this apparition out of my head and felt sure I had nearly died.

When we returned home to London I rang Mum, who then lived in Somerset. She said she was so relieved to hear I was fine as she had had a terrifying experience whilst we were there. One night she heard me calling her from outside the window of their house in Crowcombe. She heard me so clearly that she got Dad to open up the window in their bedroom to let me know she was coming downstairs. She was mystified as she knew I should be in France, but she also knew it was me outside. It was not long before we realized that both events had happened on the same night. How can one explain this? I only have this feeling with some people. People I am somehow spiritually connected with. I may not even know them that well, but there's a connection. What is this extra sense that most people do not acknowledge? I don't either. I think in my head if you have incredibly strong intuition and empathy you can more or less get inside someone else's head.

So if you are a real empath you maybe have such a heightened sense of communication that you really don't need the words or even the presence of someone else to feel when they are in trouble or to let them know when you are. I don't know. It remains a mystery. I accept seeing feathers, robins, rainbows are all projections of our desire to see a sign of hope. This fits with the positive bias that Peter Kay jokes about in the Quavers funeral. And yet.

My French escapade? Proof that Mum and I have a psychic bond, or I drank dodgy red wine with sulphites and hallucinated and Mum meanwhile was worried about me going on a foreign holiday with a relatively new boyfriend when I was rather underweight. The psychologist in me thinks the second explanation is more reasonable, but the first is entertaining.

CHAPTER 11

SOCIETY MOURNS NOT

As we have moved steadily in the west away from formalized religion, it has become inevitable that we find some way of creating a secular ritual for mourning. So vicars are replaced with registered officials who can preside over the legal formalities and the personal visit to the bereaved family or individual. To work as it were with the care of a priest but without the religious need to explain why the body was taken or where the body would go. This is a Registered Official called a Celebrant and is someone who has been trained to legally preside over a funeral and to deliver the oration. A criticism of Vicars and priests in recent times providing funeral services is that they have not really known the person in their parish who they talk about in the funeral address. There is nothing more agonizing than a Vicar waxing lyrical about someone and getting it wrong, because actually they scarcely knew them and are working with a collection of facts that they have been provided with. There is a humorous rendition of this in 'Bridget Jones' Baby' where Hugh Grant's lascivious character Daniel Cleaver is being mourned by ten rows of Eastern European ex-girlfriends. The Vicar is getting it horribly wrong to comic effect for the film's purposes. In fact the bumbling, fusty, incompetent vicar has become something of a stereotype enjoyed by us in a variety of films in recent years. Rowan Atkinson has enjoyed a stammering vicar, Dick Emery provided a buffoon vicar with goofy teeth, perhaps Dawn French has provided the most sensitive modern vicar figure that we all wish we had in our parish. And it is perhaps this model that a Funeral Celebrant is closer to. Being in touch with worldly concerns and issues, without judgement and with pastoral care. My sister is a funeral celebrant and she makes a point of really counselling the family and finding out all about the person who has died. It is then up to the family to provide her with photographs, a film, music etc., to present at the funeral in order to be in touch with who this person really was. This can be very relevant to family and friends. For non-religious families, going to a church and having a strange set of rituals with a person in authority, who may have their own judgements and lack of knowledge about the person who had died, could cause further distress. At the very least it would be hard to see how a service that a person is not used to can be comforting. I use the term non-religious in place of agnostic or atheist as the former suggests that not much thought has gone into it, which reflects how a lot of people live their lives, not a studied theoretical stand point. Just a place where religion or church going has not been a part of their upbringing.

We are comforted by what we know, what we are familiar with. So for me a church would bring comfort, but for many others it could be alienating. I was brought up going to church every week. My school had a religious service at the start of every school day (the Jewish girls went out to have their separate service and joined us gentiles for the general notices at the end of the service). So Christianity was pretty much drummed into me from as early as I can remember. Church is a place where I feel secure, I know the ritual. I know how to turn to the right bits in the prayer book at which point. I know when to kneel and when to stand. I know when to give the responses. I know the tunes of the chants and the lyrics of the hymns. As surely as a good Muslim know their creed, as a good Jew knows their rituals, I know my Christian ones. But imagine not knowing any of it? And how awful it would be to be plunging in and out of places with no particular sense in the prayer book and singing songs that you don't know the tune to? This is what it is like for so many people in secular Britain.

Church has traditionally been the embodiment of society and providing a crucial role in guidance in life. There is rarely a murder or death of a child being reported on the news without the Head Teacher and or the local Vicar talking about the family. It is to whom the media turns to for 'official' appraisal. But as society changes so does this reference. After the recent death of baby Alfie Evans it was the Chairman of Everton football club who gave something of an oration for Alfie.

Alfie had been kept on life support whilst his parents fought legal battle after legal battle in an attempt to stop the hospital switching it off. The results from all experts, including one flown over from the US who had a specialty in working with the syndrome that Alfie suffered from, all supported the hospital's view that Alfie had no hope of survival and the level of pain he was in could not be assessed. It was a heartbreaking story for everyone. For the parents who wanted to do everything and anything to hold on to him. For the rather misguided supporters who honked horns outside Alder Hey hospital as they went past. The poor devoted nurses who were depicted as being murderers but who also would have to face the pain of saying goodbye to little Alfie after they had cared for him day in and day out for over a year. But somehow Everton football club became the cathedral to which the parents turned and who led the tributes to Alfie when he died.

Indeed, Delia Smith was seduced by football when she went to her first match. Delia Smith CBE is known widely for her TV career as a no nonsense cook teaching the viewer how to make great dishes. If Delia did a recipe with filo pastry the next day Sainsbury's, Tesco's and Waitrose would sell out of it. It was known as the 'Delia Effect'. But football and in particular Norwich Football Club has been incredibly important to her as she is a joint majority shareholder of the club. She said the first time she went to a football match she found the noise was overwhelming in the ground and it felt like a massive cathedral of passion. So football has fast become our church, our cathedral, and there is scarcely a game that is played without the teams wearing black armbands in honour of a local hero, an old club member, an historic tragedy such as Hillsborough. There is a reverence that is played out on the pitch with silence or with a roar that holds more meaning for most of Britain's working class that a church does. The churches are empty or sparsely filled with silver haired ladies. But the cathedral of the football stadium is packed.

Anecdotal Testimony

There had been so many times that they thought he would die. For the last 23 years he had suffered with a stroke, a heart attack, internal hemorrhage. He had had more operations and more body parts replaced than the bionic man. He had been put in intensive care in an induced coma to try and stem a hemorrhage from his carotid artery. Jane prayed that day harder than she had ever prayed. Please God save him.

He survived many operations but his mood blunted after each one and his previous good humour was less so. Before as he always says 'he was taken' he could often be the life and soul of the party. Showing off, laughing, asking interesting questions of people. Even though she was his daughter, Jane would always want to be around him at a party. He would be her favourite person to sit next to at the table. She enjoyed his company and he enjoyed hers.

After 'he was taken' it became progressively hard to remember that personality that shone for so many years. Existent personality traits came to the fore, that Jane had noticed but not dwelt on before. Suddenly in old age and ill, these less laudable character traits seemed dominant. So much so Jane had to do a lot of deep breathing before she entered his bedroom. The moaning, groaning, woe is me was quite exhausting. Why couldn't he just suck it up and stop complaining. Sometimes now, looking back on that time, when she was an inexpert nurse, she feels guilt. I was so intolerant. I shouldn't have shouted at him that time. I shouldn't have bitched about him to my sisters. Then other times she still has to share how awfully difficult it was looking after him. He was such a strong personality that he couldn't stand being told what to do. He always thought he knew better. Most of his life he had known better. But imperceptibly towards the end she knew better. But he would not accept this change of dynamics. He was still her father and she would dance to his tune. When we didn't he was depressed or furious. The more difficult he became, the less he was listened to. Which is where an old person can become like a stroppy toddler.

It depressed Jane to see him in this state. When he had gone into the nursing home she visited him out of duty. She tried to re-engage him in their old routine. Sometimes she saw a glimmer of his humour again. Sometimes she could talk and he would actually listen. He still could ask questions about the family and his grandchildren. He knew who everyone was and how they interconnected, but to sustain a conversation though was too difficult. There would be intrusions, like searching for a radio channel. You could hear a channel clearly and then the shrill sound of it being lost and the white noise of radio space.

He was kept alive for a long time. His mind and body wasting away in equal measure. It was distressing to see. Each time Jane saw him she would find it harder and harder to shake this image of an old dying man out of her head and to remember the one she loved so much and enjoyed being around. Her sister said she needed to visit as he really was ready to go and just wanted to say goodbye to her and check everything was alright. So Jane flew to the UK to the nursing home and her father sipped a cup of coffee through a straw held by her. It was his last drink. A heavy dose of morphine was given to him and he fell into a deep sleep. Jane and her sister sat there reading Hello magazines and OK magazines, discussing characters featuring in the glossy pages. It was the kind of conversation they would have had years ago in the living room and their Dad listening to it hopefully would have felt comforted by its normality. The nurses had told them that the last thing to go is hearing, so that it would be reassuring for him to hear them chatting away. Jane left the home before he died. The nursing staff were with him as he took his last breath. She didn't want to see him die.

CHAPTER 12

PLACE OF MEMORY, THE DEATH OF PRINCESS DIANA

Traditionally in the UK graveyards and crematoriums are where souls are laid to rest and a tombstone with words of comfort, or biography will be testament to the loss of the person. Graves are reassuring places in many ways because they are a solid statement and reminder that this person did exist. So on a birthday or at Christmas or whenever there is a meaningful time when a family or individual wants to talk to, or pay respect to someone they miss, they can have a pilgrimage to the grave. Flowers can be left in place. This scene is used widely in drama in films, in books. The scene where the character talks to the person through the grave as it were. Then, just as in Greek tragedy, another character will turn up at the same time and there will be some sort of recognition scene. So this anchor, this stone and reference is firmly rooted in our cultural history. But when Princess Diana died this cultural reference point was turned on its head. There was a revolution overnight in how we mourned as a nation and how we made our pilgrimage. It wasn't to a grave. We didn't have a grave and the one that was finally made had to be hidden, secret and inaccessible. So humans being humans, they found a way to demonstrate their love and their loss.

Kensington Palace became engulfed in a sea of flowers. People made a pilgrimage to London to show their respects. Diana had not died there. But people felt that this was a place she loved and that was there they could pay homage to her. And pay homage they did. With bouquet after bouquet of flowers. It was something the country had never seen before. My father, a historian, had a rather blunt response to it. It was mass hysteria and anyway she had died young and beautiful and no one would ever be able to take that away from her. I disagreed. I don't think it was mass hysteria. I think it was more mass anger and feeling desperately sad for her and the boys.

I was not in the country when she died. I was in France in hospital having my appendix taken out. Princess Diana was the same age as me. So I always looked at what she was having to deal with and felt people expected an awful lot more of her than other young women. She wasn't perfect by any means. That why we loved her. Because she knew she wasn't perfect but she still tried her best for people who had less than her. She grew within her role. And when I came around from my operation and was being helped to the loo by the nurses they said, 'Votre Princess e mort' (Your Princess is dead). I can remember collapsing with shock and begging them to tell me what they meant. From then on for a week in hospital I could not stop crying. I just sobbed and sobbed. The nurses in Dax hospital were not sympathetic. The French driver died too you know, we can be sad for him. It was before the finger of blame had been pointed at him. Yes. the anti-monarchist tradition was still embroidered into the tapestry of French sentiment. They told me off for crying so much and told me to pull myself together, particularly in front of my small children when they visited! They referred to me as 'l'anglaise qui pleure toute la journee'

When I was able to leave the hospital I went back to our campsite in Le Vieux Port on the Aquitaine coast to recover. It was predominantly filled with Brits and their families for a beach filled holiday with Haven children's clubs. The funeral of Princess Diana was shown in the main bar. As the hearse was paraded down the Mall with the young princes walking with their father (Prince Charles), Uncle (Charles Althorp) and Grandfather (Prince Phillip), there was not a dry eye in the place. Grown men, muscles bulging, tattooed, sobbed into their beers. They wailed with grief. We weren't even in our country. We were not getting a constant line of TV whipping us up into grief. Yes, we didn't really know her of course, but she represented something to us that hit us hard. Our English Rose, our People's Princess was gone.

I lose count of the amount of people who tried to detract from the reality of our collective grief. Sir Nicholas Soames was one of them. I wondered if the stiff upper lip brigade felt threatened by us being so very not British and wailing like lunatics over her death. A few years later I had moved to Luxembourg and had met a Welsh woman that would become a close friend. We were in the process of buying two fish tanks in Hornbach (think Wickes DIY) to basically do a school project our sons had been given, creating a miniature version of a water cycle. As we got to the cash point we got onto the 'where were you when Princess Diana died?' conversation. Within five minutes, two women who scarcely knew each other bar a couple of coffees at our sons' school, were sobbing in a car park outside a DIY shop in Luxembourg. Mass hysteria, no. It was a phenomenon I would venture. The likes of which we are unlikely to see again.

CHAPTER 13

DYING ON SOCIAL MEDIA

It is now considered acceptable by many to announce a death on social media. With the large amount of traffic and the extent of its reach, some etiquette has been worked through on various sites. These recommend waiting for at least 24 hours before announcing it, making sure that all close family members and friends already know personally before it is posted. It is recommended that few details of how the person actually died are revealed, just the minimum, as if in a newspaper notification of death. The etiquette is for friends to wait until either the partner or parents of the deceased has made a post and those closest to the deceased, before making a post. There is advice about posting a picture up of you and the deceased in the place of words if you cannot think of the right thing to say.

This framework helping people not to make terrible gaffs is a good idea. But sadly, having had several young people die from the school at which my children attended, young people don't necessarily pay attention to etiquette. And I don't imagine anyone cares either. Because the young are so used to using social media more than anyone and they seem to understand the rules better than the wrinklies or 'the Jims' as I believe we are known. That is parents who think they are tech savvy and use social media a lot.

What has happened is that the deceased young person's Facebook profile page becomes a sort of grave to place flowers, or the gates of Kensington Palace. The profile page has become the mecca to which people turn with their outpouring of love and sadness. Of course with the loss of a young person's life there is a tragic emotion that is felt by all. A bit like wailing and screaming as a ritual in the middle east, I get the sense that young people gather at the Facebook page and commiserate with memories and funny photos and prop each other up. For an older person there is something quite uncomfortable about this. Almost macabre. But for the young it brings a sort of normality and a reference point to look at. Like an old album of photos or an old diary. But in a positive way for them as it is interactive.

I find the Facebook page of a dead person with no reference to them being dead as very odd. So that this person finds immortality on the net. Maybe people who have been very affected by this person have a need to keep them alive. An immortality on the web. In USA Today on Feb 12, 2015 Donna Leinwand Leger reported on the new Facebook policy which allows social media immortality. Now Facebook will allow someone to manage a posthumous page. It is called a legacy page. 'Death may take your body, but it doesn't have to extinguish your online persona.'

So how does it work? In the US users can choose a 'legacy contact' to make one last post on your behalf when you die. That contact can respond to new friend requests, update the cover photo and profile, and archive your Facebook posts and photos. Previously FB would memorialize the account, meaning it could be viewed but not changed or added to. It was in response to a huge demand of requests that prompted the change. People wanted to let other people know of a memorial service, post photos etc.

There is a practical application of course in terms of arranging a party or memorial service. Previously reported in the local newspaper or in a broad sheet, but now the reach is more widespread. You don't have to read the same paper. There is also the possibility of sharing much loved photos amongst friends and family. But taking over the decision of accepting new friends or contacts seems deeply troubling. It reminds me of Natalie Cole creating an album with her Dad when he was already dead. Cutting and splicing her voice into his music. The general feeling is that he would have loved it. But do we really know? The person is dead and has no control over any future decision. I feel there is a boundary that should not be overstepped.

An American friend's husband fought a long battle with cancer. He was always very candid about what he was going through on his Facebook page. Now his wife writes on it. First anniversary without you my darling. I looked up at the fireworks and knew you were with me. Another post she sees a double rainbow on Valentine's Day and know he has sent it. It is touching how her emotions are seeing signs. Signs that everyone else will also see and apportion meaning to. But for her she only sees her husband in heaven watching over her and sending her a sign.

But the human heart has an amazing ability to see some meaning wherever they look. Despite science repeatedly failing to find any validity in mediums or psychics. Humans have a need for religion, for an afterlife and for a relevance that appeals to their narcissistic needs.

CHAPTER 14

LIVING ON

Returning again to our desire for immortality, but not in a religious sense, our secular world tries to cling on to life. Films depicting mothers dying leaving books for their baby about how much they loved them. Leaving presents for every birthday they would have until they are 18, so they would never forget how much their mother loved them. Maybe this legacy for the child is therapeutic, but there is a mawkish feeling to it. Children have resilience built into their developmental DNA. Being more vulnerable in nature, children can exhibit quite callous behavior in order to survive. An ability to grab what is required. Empathy comes in at a later stage developmentally and selflessness later still. So as sad as it is when a mother dies young and leaves behind a grieving husband and small child, would it not be healthier to hope that he could move on with a loving woman who could become a caring step mum to the child. I cannot help feeling that 6 years in to a new marriage that a birthday with some dated gift from the dead mother would be uncomfortable. Almost like a ghost in the house. It speaks volumes to me of the need of the dying mother to hold on to her position as mother. It's understandable, but yet is it right? Is it right to attempt to invent new ways of staying on earth when you are not? Why is there such a need to control every variable in the one area where the variable cannot be controlled? If you believe in God and heaven then you can lift it up to him and relax knowing that it is all taken care of. You don't have to worry. Our mortal toil on earth is nothing in comparison to what is to come. And if there is no eternal life, then we just die and we will not know anything more about it. The only people who will suffer are the people left behind. So these attempts to take control of the inevitable seem to people who do not want to accept not living on. Religion has been rejected, whichever religion they culturally would be part of, but in the absence of God taking care of things there is a frantic attempt to take care of it themselves.

And in the example of the mother leaving all the notes to her daughter or son, yes it's an outpouring of her love, but it is frozen in time. It is frozen at the moment that she is dying or knows that she is dying. The love that she feels is for a baby or a young child. With each year that passes the child develops their personality and life experience. The mother can only refer to her feelings of maternal love. The developing child, adolescent and young woman or man is not known to her. It can never be known. It's a leap to trust but letting go seems so much healthier. Yes, leave a letter of love, but just one. And trust the father to tell stories to the child about their mother which will always help the child to know who she or he came from. The laughs that they had, the good and the bad, not an idealized image. I recall the film 'Letters from my Mother' which my sister and I watched on a 'duvet day' as children. Duvet days were days where we both professed to be sick on the same day so that we could keep each other company and binge watch Hallmark type films on TV. Normally Lassie films were our sob fest, but on this occasion we made the mistake of watching this film about a mother who left a box of letters to her daughter to open after her death. As a child I think one is much more sensitive to the fear of losing one's mother, or of death in general, it seems the ultimate sadness. And so we sat and watched this film which really went for it in terms of misery. The music swelling with each moment of blatant sentimentality and sadness. We were rocking with sobs, punching the sofa with misery and then intermittently as we caught site of each other getting appalling giggles. This emotional range we have carried on into adulthood and we exhibited in Intensive Care with our father and at the funeral of our mother. Why high emotion with uncontrolled sobbing and helpless giggles are so linked with us I do not know, but I have heard others describe the same phenomenon.

So when you know you are dying, as tragic as it is, it seems to me that trusting in some higher being to help accept death and a life that you have no real control over existing after you have gone. We are human and cannot control events when we are gone. With a wish and a prayer is the best we can really hope for.

CHAPTER 15

A GOOD DEATH

Grayson Perry looks at the idea of a good death in his series *'Grayson Perry: Rites of Passage'* on Channel 4. A man suffering from a motor neuron disease wants to take his moment when he is ready and die and he wants to be the guest of honour at his own funeral. His wife supports him in this. He says to Grayson that death used to frighten him, but having suffered with MND for 9 years he wants to get it over and done with. He says that if he takes his breathing apparatus off it would take 4 to 5 days for him to die.

His life clearly has been quite a blokey affair, with pub life and high jinks and devoted family. He decides to hold his funeral before he dies. This takes our obsession with quirky and innovative messing with tradition to new heights. Grayson Perry makes him an urn which friends come up to and put gifts into. In much the same way as Pharaohs were buried with jewels and treats in their pyramids, so the friends and family are putting stuff in for him to enjoy in the after-life. There is a lot of humour involved in the presents. Plenty of drink goes in, cigars, the wife throws in her wedding garter. So the man enjoys seeing how much he is loved and how much he was appreciated. Somehow they all seem to hold it together, although how much self-control must have been involved I do not know. It was a lovely goodbye to him. But it was not a funeral. Grayson Perry helps design the service with the urn to help him have a really 'good death', but is this a good death, is there any good death except not being in too much pain, not attempting to control it and knowing little of it?

A funeral is not for the dead it is for the living. It is where they can sob. It's where they do not have to hold it together for the person dying. It is where society gives us permission to be sad. The family and friends gather together to go through this ritual. We know the score. We know how to behave. We can cry and hug our friends and family. Funerals have a purpose either in a religious sense or in a societal sense. It is a rite of passage to have a funeral, a burial or internment of ashes.

Levi-Strauss, Claude introduced the theory of structuralism. As a philosopher and anthropologist, Levi-Strauss studied the commonalities of structure within tribes and society. He found structuralism could explain language and shared myths. If you don't look at the detail, but the role of objects and people within myths, they rarely vary in content. Psychologists have used this kind of analysis in conversation analysis, where gaps and words are coded. Levi-Strauss found language, myths and even human thought seemed to follow some sort of Universal Law. This is the system that he worked with to analyse how as social beings we interact and celebrate and make sense of our world.

Religion is an archaic and still existent form of making sense of life. If we use a structure such as a powerful being sending weather patterns and diseases and taking life and then allow ourselves to think in terms of our action being accountable to this greater being, then not only is social order more likely to be kept, but also in smaller communities, ethical boundaries can be upheld. The interaction between survival of humans and rules applied to communities is generally rooted in science. The incest taboo helps prevent deformed babies and encourages outward breeding with other tribes, peoples. Somehow nature makes sure that we look to others for sexual trysts. In Judaism eating pork was and still is forbidden. In ancient Israel eating pork would have been a risky business as it would have been prone to giving you diseases or food poisoning. So religion took care of the science. We humans tend to need a structure that tells us what to do for our own benefit. With religion becoming increasingly unpopular society struggles to fill the void that it leaves. A friend of mine who was a local GP in the Suffolk village we lived in said that Doctors are the new priests. He said that so many of his patients came to him, not for a visible illness, but to confess essentially and get some sort of absolution. Dr 'I am worried about watching so much porn. It's like an obsession'. So instead of being sent off to do 10 Hail Mary's the doctor chats through with the guy and tries to make him feel a little less guilty and make some changes to his behavior. He was convinced this was why doctors are so overworked. Half the appointments he reckoned could be dealt with by a priest. In a similar fashion a lot of my work as a Psychotherapist would traditionally been conducted by a priest or vicar. Marital woes, infidelity I found frequently the client was really asking for help in deciding whether to stay or go. Of course I imagine a vicar would encourage them to stay, and certainly a priest would, but as a therapist you really have to present the decision to the client. Help them really mull over the choices and help them to do what they really want to do. Despite never telling a client to either leave a marriage or to dump a lover, the client would be able to tell the wife/husband/lover that their therapist had told them they had to finish it. I know this to be the case. So it is easier to hide behind a figure to help make a difficult decision. Therapy in these circumstances helps the client come to terms with the decision they have probably already made.

So we want to abandon our faith but we need something to fill the void. There are therapists and doctors and meditation, but when it comes to death its so overwhelming none of these religious substitutes can really help. And so there is this head long panic in an effort to control either an idea that this person is still somewhere and watching over you, or that they are simply no more.

CHAPTER 16

WHAT ARE THE IMPLICATIONS OF BEING JUST SIMPLY DEAD?

I recently took my cat, aged 18, to the vet to be euthanized. I did not take the decision lightly. I had hoped like most pet owners do that my lovely Domino would die gently in her sleep. But after 4 days of not eating and only sipping at water, lying limply with her head turned into her basket, I knew that she was near the end and that she must be suffering. As I held her in her little bed, my senses were assailed by her foul smelling breath. It was gut wrenchingly awful. A visceral smell of death coming up from within her. I was gagging and had to breathe through my mouth to prevent the gagging. I felt distraught for my lovely cat and emotional that I was taking her to her death. There was a mixture of protectiveness and helplessness.

Arriving at the vets she quickly assessed by the green gunk in my cat's mouth that she was nearly there. She was given a sedative and that induced a vomit. Once that was over the vet offered for me to leave the room. I felt I should be there at her death. That somehow it would be remiss and cowardly to leave before she died. And so I stroked her gently as the vet delivered the fatal injection. And that was it. She was dead. And within the space of a few minutes my emotions had gone from high anxiety to seeing a fluffy object on the vet's table.

If I'm honest the overriding feeling was one of relief. Yes, I miss her meowing at the door to be fed. I miss her scuttling out of the kitchen when she knows she shouldn't be there. The funny way my dog and she used to carry on when I was out of the house, curled up by the fire and sleeping on the white sofas cushions they both knew they were not allowed on. But seeing her in pain and struggling to live was awful. And now she's just gone. She's had her time alive and now she is simply dead. I don't believe she's crossed a rainbow bridge or that she is in cat heaven. I believe she is dead and that animals just die. Once the flow in the body stops then there is degradation and then the body becomes an inanimate object.

A lot of people feel distressed by this notion. Other people find it comforting. People who have been indoctrinated into the idea of Hell, such as the Pentecostal Church and Catholics, can be absolutely terrified of Hell and eternal damnation. Who would not be terrified of an eternity of fire and punishment with screaming ghouls? That is what hell is described as. When we sleep and have nightmares we can feel stuck in something that thankfully when we wake up we can explain to ourselves was simply a nightmare. There is that feeling that after a particularly bad nightmare that the feeling returns during the day. As the details of what the actual nightmare are forgotten during the day, some essence of the bad feeling keeps rearing up. One tries to make sense of it, but it's an emotional feeling rather than a reality so we just try and suppress the feeling. In some ways I could imagine that this is what hell could be like. But it is hard to see how any emotional capacity could be left once the body is no longer animated. This is where the logic of science, the experience of seeing the difference between even a very sick being and a dead being, seems to throw the idea of an afterlife into serious doubt. And would not an end to pain and suffering and thought be a release? The sadness and the pain is with the living.

Diana Athill writes about ageing, in *'Somewhere towards the End'* about the things that we do not say and maybe the young cannot know. They are worth sharing and her treatment of approaching death is as logical as is her writing. It is honest. *'...and if you have been, or are being, exceptionally lucky you naturally make the most of that, but 'at my back I always hear / Time's winged chariot hurrying near', and that is sobering, to say the least of it.'*

She notes how people who have had children leave their genes, people who have created something leave that behind. Which is why she does not believe that atheists need think their existence has been for naught, but that how they have lived their life is of utmost importance.

'What dies is not a life's value, but the worn-out (or damaged) container of the self, together with the self's

awareness of itself: away that goes into nothingness, with everyone else's.'

The puzzle of death is a question for all of us. Diana does not shirk from its reality. *"a person who is just about to die is still fully alive and fully her or himself – I remember thinking as I sat beside my mother 'But she can't be dying, because she's still so entirely here' (the wonderful words which turned out to be her last, 'It was absolutely divine', were not intended as such but were just part of something she was telling me). The difference between being and non-being is both so abrupt and so vast that it remains shocking even though it happens to every living thing that is, was, or ever will be"*

This fact that she lays out as basically and as clearly as she can. It's an unavoidable complication of living as of course as my father would say. She slight scoffs at Henry James calling death 'distinguished', *'when it is the commonest thing in life, I can't imagine – though the poor old man was at his last gasp when he said it, so one ought not to carp'*

She ends with last words, suitably enough. She is sad that not being religious she won't be able to say *'Dieu me pardonnerai, c'est son métier'* but would like to say *'It's all right. Don't mind not knowing'*. And here she references her fear, the same way we all have a fear if we are honest, and she accepts that she still hopes her death does not come soon.

As I mention I could take my cat to be euthanized as a dignified end to her life. She was my pet but also an animal. Her functions very typical of all cats. She had a delicate gait, would knead a cushion to get cosy, would prance and dance in the garden. She would stalk her prey and play with a mouse or small bird mercilessly. My Dog I think I will struggle more with. So devoted a friend and the loyalty of a Labrador to their owner is like none other. But still I remain blessed by years of playing on a farm and developing something of the farmers' modus operandi. Keep your animals healthy and happy and safe until you send them off to slaughter. Of course, a dog is a pet, not a source of income, but still keeping them healthy and knowing when to let them go is part of being a responsible owner.

With the Disney films and popular culture animals have increasingly been given human characteristics that simply are false. You only have to look at the rather cruel set ups on YouTube where an owner does a sort of dialogue to a dog and the poor dog has to respond to various commands as if they are a human responding with embarrassment etc. Utter hogwash and I find it quite cruel and exploitative. This has extended into a lot of other hogwash of going over the rainbow bridge to play in heaven with all the other dogs etc. I find it nonsense and of course one does not comment as the owner expressing this stuff is finding their way of mourning. It's not the time to make your point. In America very elaborate services are now available. A woman who sadly could not conceive, formed an extraordinarily close bond with her Red Setter. When he finally died the loss was as if it were her child. She had a special cremation with the ashes returned in an urn with gold imprint of the dog's paw prints. Quite cute I guess for her, a memory to hold on to, a first world excess.

Having said that I have had numerous clients who have had grief therapy for dealing with the death of their dogs. It is quite amazing how these animals wiggle their way into our hearts and lives, so that when they die many owners are totally bereft. One reason I think it is particularly hard is because they are always like small children, dependent on you, therefore there is this feeling of their reliance on you to make things better. When you cannot, there is an inevitable sense of having left them down. One client described the noises in the house. She said she would hear the scrape of a dish and think it was her dog having food or water in the kitchen and then she would have to remind herself that those noises were gone now forever. There was something extremely moving about her description of the noises that disappear when a pet dies.

CHAPTER 17

HELPING SOMEONE TO DIE

In the UK, rising numbers of dying patients in Hospices presented a strain on nurses and on their families. With the advantages of so many interventions in medicine to keep someone alive artificially or longer than 'God intended', a care policy was put in place famously in Liverpool, called 'The Liverpool Care Pathway for the Dying Patient' Jane Seymour wrote a paper analysing its rise, demise and legacy in England. It was discontinued in 2014.

The Integrated Care Pathway (ICP) was recommended by successive governments in England and Wales to improve end of life care. It came from the hospice context and was extended throughout the country before it was suddenly withdrawn.

'The epidemiology of dying is also changing. Increasingly for many, death will follow an extended period of uncertainty, frailty and multiple morbidity in advanced old age. In contrast the rapidly progressing downward trajectory of dying with it clear point of entry to the dying phase, which was central to the original hospice model of cancer palliative care...'

LCP was first described in a publication in 1997 as a means of transferring key principles taken from hospice care into general health care settings such as hospitals and care homes.   After mounting criticism the government implemented a national review led by Baroness Julia Neuberger in 2013. It was abruptly taken off the table in 2014 leading to polarized views.

Allen and Rixson stroke care cite the aim of the integrated pathways as being *'....the right people, doing the right things, in the right order, at the right time, in the right place, with the right outcome' (p. 81)*

Allen described Integrated care pathways as 'classic examples' (p.305) of boundary objects because they straddle clinical, managerial and user interests.

The LCP was formulated during the 1990s at the Royal Liverpool University Hopitals NHS Trust and the Marie Curie Hospice in Liverpool. LCP was focused on patients and the dying phase (described as the last 48 hours of life).

'The patients is bedridden, the patient is semi-comatose; the patient is able only to take sips of fluids; the patient is no longer able to take tablets'

A template for use addressing 4 domains of care: physical, psychological, social and spiritual. In 2000 a National Cancer Plan was published by the government as part of its, NHS modernization programme to improve the care of the dying to the level of the best. (para 7.21).

LCP became something of a gold standard as how it could be done published in NICE (National Institute of Clinical Excellence) in 2004 (para 8.33). The LCP brought together communicating with patient and family, planning for psychosocial and spiritual needs, symptom control such as pain control, agitation and respiratory tract secretions and care after death including leaflets for relatives.

The reason for its withdrawal was that there was no evidenced based data for establishing positive death. If LCP accepted as a gold standard everywhere when it is untested, we will then be unable to test its efficacy, as ethical approval will be almost impossible (p.197 to 8).
There was sadness amongst those who pioneered the LCP and who felt that it had the right components to transition a patient through the death process with the right people playing the right roles in the right order. However, perhaps with ever increasing lawsuits appearing in the NHS in the UK, the care package seemed no longer empirically safe to continue with in other contexts.

In reality helping someone to die still happens. A strong dose of morphine eases the inevitable passage of death. Not in a Harold Shipman way, but just a pain relief that eases an otherwise inevitable process. I still wonder though how hard it must be for the Doctors who administer this treatment. It's all very well for us family to be relieved that the Doctor is easing our loved one into death, but we do not have the responsibility for doing it ourselves. I wonder how many of us would be prepared to do it. Even with the ghastly death penalty in the US there are several doses activated so that no one individual has the responsibility of knowing they murdered the convict. It distances them from the ultimate sin of taking a life. With a Doctor, it is not murder of course. The same dose of morphine would not affect a normal healthy person, but certainly in a very weakened dying patient, it will carry them off. It must be hard to deliver that dose. I dwell on this point and maybe this reveals my underlying religious belief, that maybe there is heaven and hell and maybe this could be a game changer. Maybe this action would be considered not an act of mercy but a sin. Not letting God choose when a life is taken, but using the power to do no harm, implicit in the Hippocratic Oath, to speed up death.

Actual Testimony

Her father had been an alcoholic most of her young life. Aged only 5 and with three older siblings, her mother decided that whilst she loved her husband, the family home was no place for him due to his drinking behavior. Her mother wanted Jane to be able to share as much of the positive side of her father as she could.

There was no desire to prevent him from having a positive relationship with his children. But she had to protect him and them from seeing each other when he was on a drinking binge. Jane thought little of it, being so young, but it was a pattern of alcohol withdrawal, sobriety and then falling into alcohol abuse again. So she only ever saw her father when he was sober. He was a great walker and would go walking with her and her sisters. Jane loves to cook and this she believes was inherited from her father. Whether she loved to source food on their walks because she made this association with him, or whether they both had that sensual gene for finding good food and enjoying its taste, it's hard to decide. Like most nature/ nurture arguments, it's almost certainly a compelling combination. Jane describes her walks with her Dad where they would pick nettles and then take their bounty home and cook Nettle Soup. Of course, it would taste tremendous. From the earth to their stomachs.

During her teenage years there were times when, understanding his alcoholism now more, she felt angry towards him. Why doesn't he love me enough to stay sober so he can see me more often. Why am I not worthy of that? And meanwhile the tortured addict attempted repeatedly to live a sober life.

Her father used to go for long walks with a good friend and it was after one of these that he went missing. For four days he was missing until his body was found on a moor. Finally his drinking had killed him and his tortured soul could stop the fight. Jane was clearing his stuff up in his house and found a tragic note listing reasons to stay sober. Of course seeing his children was number one on the list. Achieving more at work, not having hangovers. It was a painful reminder of how strong addiction is. There's no logic to it. It's just a driving force that overrides all others. So hard for a child to understand. Or indeed a wife.

Jane was relieved that she had recently, after a period of annoyed silence, decided to send him a birthday card. She told him how much she loved him and how much he meant to her. She had a great sense of relief that she had done that. What is extraordinary is how her Mother handled the situation. Somehow, despite the shocking nature of his addiction and ultimate death, she presented her father as a good man to be respected and loved.

CHAPTER 18

PILGRIMAGE

Pilgrims have long walked and meditated and prayed as they make their way towards a monument or place of miracle. Muslims flock to Mecca, a city in the Hejazi region of Saudi Arabia. The Haji (Pilgrimage) is held in the 12th Muslim lunar month of Dhul-Hijjah. It is the birthplace of Muhammad, a cave 3 km from Mecca and the site of Muhammad's first revelation of the Quran. It is obligatory for all able Muslims to make a pilgrimage to the Kaaba at least once in their lifetime, the holiest site of the Muslim religion and the direction to which all Muslims pray. It is an act of service, rather than for personal gain

But in itself it is being a good Muslim which means that when you end your earthly life you then begin your afterlife. Death is seen as the separation of the soul from the body. The Quran and Islamic literature does not shy away from dealing with death and its meaning. One idea is that the angel of death appears to the dying to take out their souls. The sinners' souls are taken out in the most painful way, while a good Muslim has their soul extracted easily.

After the burial, two angels called Munkar and Nakir come to question the dead in order to test their faith. The righteous believers answer well and live in peace whilst the bad Muslim answers badly or incorrectly and is punished. Suicide, euthanasia and unjust murder as means of death are all prohibited in Islam and are considered major sins.

In this way, that life on earth is a test by God for living after death is much the same as a Christian doctrine. And the judgement day has parallels with the Christian faith as well. That God will come to judge every individual on resurrection day.

When a Muslim is dying, they must say 'I testify that there is no god but Allah, and Muhammed is the messenger of Allah'

A Catholic is read the last rights which are meant to prepare the dying person's soul for death by absolving sins and by penance, sacramental grace and prayers for the relief of suffering through anointing and the final administration of the Eucharist "Viaticum" (Latin meaning *with you on the way*).

Tony Mariot, Researcher Biblical Antiquities at University of Oxford (2009-present) explains:

'The Roman Catholic sacrament of anointing of the sick or extreme unction is performed on a seriously ill person for spiritual and physical strength, or when a person is close to death as preparation for heaven. The priest anoints the sick person with oil and prays over him.

When combined with confession and the Eucharist, it is called 'Last Rites'...The Roman Catholic Church states that this sacrament can be repeatedly used during the long course of an ongoing illness and that it should be used before serious surgery.'

This idea is that almost like an insurance policy, but absolutely vital for safe transition through death. But there is also a feeling that during a long illness that peace and relief can be found through a religious leader giving the last rites.

In the Musee protestant the history of the protestant attitude towards death is discussed. The burial ceremony in the 16th century was minimal but in the 19th century gained more of an occasion, but intended for the living, not for the deceased. In old Israel resurrection did not exist, but later on when Hebrews were exiled in Babylon, Persian influence led to the notion of resurrection. First century Jews began to hope for resurrection but it was not until later and the development of the New Testament that the idea of resurrection became associated with Protestantism. And then it was linked to the end of the world, judgment day.

Thessalonians ch. 4 'I would have that ye sorrow not, evan as others which have no hope...the Lord himself shall descend from heaven...and those who have died in Christ shall rise first. Then we, and the living who remain, shall be caught up together with them, to meet the Lord in the clouds'

From the 15th century a 'danse macabre' was seen in murals in churches, chapels and galleries surrounding cemeteries. It showed death as a skeleton which led people of every age in a frantic dance. The art depicted reflected fear of in Europe at that time of famine, war and plague after the 14th century.

The rules became that paradise for those worthy of being saved, hell for those who deserved to be damned and purgatory for those in between such states, where they could purify themselves before going to Paradise (doctrine of the Council of Lyon in 1274)

So in seeking redemption pilgrimages became popular to ensure their salvation, particularly popular on the to do list were Jerusalem, Rome or Saint James of Compostela.
After the Reformation a distinction between Protestantism and Catholicism became that free salvation given by God and not related to merit. They now believed that salvation had been given to all Christians through Christ. So being good should be in gratitude to God, not as a self-serving act.

Luther proposed an idea of an afterlife either in communion with God or separated from God following life on earth. He did not commit to ideas about the soul. On the other hand Calvin thought the immortality of the soul as crucially a characteristic of man, separating us from animals. At the end of time God would give men's bodies back to their souls.

Protestants believed that Christ had told them there should only be two sacraments baptism and the Lord's supper and that for the living. Burials were to be subdued and everything given up to the power of God, so no need for a pastor to attend. The Reformed Church went further away from Catholic practices and forbade eulogizing the deceased. A pastor should not pray or preach during burials and no bells should be rung. So a burial was modest and superstitious practices were rejected. God would take care of it all. But families were fed up as they didn't get a chance to honour their deceased and it soon became clear that there was such a sense of loss that people might turn to Catholicism. A bit like a lost business opportunity. So they decided to give services to those left behind but still with no eulogy for the departed by the pastor. The body does not enter the church but is buried first in the cemetery and then the service is taken in the Temple.

Even burial of protestants ran into trouble during the 17th century as they were not permitted to be buried in cemeteries. Thus under cover of night protestants took to burying their dead in their gardens, or in a field or in their basements.

Pentecostalism started in Los Angeles but rapidly spread throughout America and the south, and the rest of the world. Mixing with Protestants and the Charismatic movement within the Protestant church the numbers have swelled throughout the world. The central belief of classical Pentecostalism is that through the death, burial and resurrection of Jesus Christ, sins can be forgiven and humanity reconciled with God. This is the 'good news'. To become Pentecostal you need to be born again. Pentecostals believe in a literal heaven and hell, heaven for those who have accepted God's gift of salvation and hell for those who have rejected it. Baptism needs also to incorporate a baptism with the Holy Spirit with Jesus Christ the agent and the Holy Spirit is the medium. The belief is that at the moment a person is born again they have the presence of the Holy Spirit within them. They believe that healing is possible through prayer and faith.

There is also a belief of an imminent second coming 'Eschatology'. Pentecostalists believe in speaking in tongues. Frequently in church there is an open casket and family and friends can file past to pay their respects to the deceased. The funeral ceremony is much the same as in any other Protestant church with a sermon, hymns and prayers, although the church is likely to be livelier and the music more vibrant.

CHAPTER 19

SUICIDE

Taking your own life used to be treated with taboo in Western Culture. I recall a girl in my church whose Father died. I asked my Mother what he had died of and she told me he had committed suicide. My Mother explained that the family did not want people in the community to know this as they would become the centre of speculation. I thought it odd at the time, because there was a lot of speculation because the service which mentioned his death seemed to be bursting with darkness and heavy with shame. There are still allusions to suicide. In the papers there might be an article referring to the death of a famous actress, aged 30, found in her home. Police do not believe there are any suspicious circumstances etc. The actress had long suffered bouts of depression. The implication is clearly embedded in the print that she had committed suicide. But somehow the human need for explanation then fuels the how was it done, who found the body, was there a note left etc. In many ways this thirst for information is somehow to avoid contamination by the event. If it was done this way, we think our son/daughter would not do it like that. Or there would have been warnings. Or if we know it to be a certain set of circumstances we can avoid being contaminated by this worst of deaths.

There is some interesting correlation with cultural influence and suicide. America could be termed as being a guilt culture. There is a lot of emphasis on making the right choices. That we develop an internal locus of control and of good behavior and expectation. If we grossly screw up in terms of our expectations, which have been culturally developed within us through parental guidance, school and church, then we feel so guilty that there are people who are unable to deal with it. It is socially developed, but it becomes an internalized state in an individual.

In a shame culture there are standard expectations of conduct. Japan is such a culture. The rate of suicide is comparatively high. A lot of suicide can be traced to economic decline or loss of jobs. Culturally there is a long history of certain suicides as being the honorable way out. The *seppuku* was the use of a short sword for self-disembowelment practiced by Samurai warriors to avoid dishonor in defeat. *Kamikaze* was flying into the enemy during World War II. This idea is at odds with the American individualistic mentally and internal locus of action. The Japanese culture puts country and others before the self. To do otherwise would inflict shame upon your family. Some people view suicide not as the taboo subject in the West, but being an almost esthetic experience and morally responsible act. This could not be more at odds with our view of suicide which is often thought of as the most selfish and cowardly act. Japan has a state called *amae* which is the need to be dependent on and accepted by others. Acceptance and conformity are more highly valued than individuality.

However, there is a recent craze in Japan for internet groups to form, who do not previously know each other, who plan to all commit suicide at the same time. This is seen as deeply dishonourable in Japan. This is not honourable deaths to atone for shame, but seen more as a fetish and as such self-serving.

A researcher called Ozawa de-Silva however argues that the deaths are explained by people who are suffering *'severe existential suffering, a loss of the "worth of living" (ikigai).....and a profound loneliness and lack of connection with others'*

(Osawa-de Silvza, Chikako (December 2008) 'Too lonely to die alone: Internet Suicide Pacts and Existential Suffering in Japan" Culture, Medicine and Psychiatry. 32 (4): 516-551)

We now have Islamic suicide bombers. The suicide bomber kills themselves and others in the belief that they are dying for the cause of Allah and that by virtue of their action they will have great rewards in the afterlife. Although it is similar to the honour deaths for the greater good in Japanese military history, it in fact taps into self-interest. The individual is persuaded to sacrifice their life in order to be rewarded with virgins and plentitude in the afterlife.

One might look at the honour control mechanism as a way of controlling vast populations and that lives are cheaper and more expendable. It could be a social construct in terms of supply and demand.

Having mentioned the work of the Japanese researcher Osawa-de-Silva, who argued that mass suicide or collective suicide by internet link was explainable in terms of existential hopelessness, it could be argued that Maslow's pyramid of needs is at play. So with self-actualisation being at the top of the pyramid when all basic and mental needs are fulfilled. We need to be fed, to be safe, to have sex and to belong. Those are the basic needs of a human being. After these conditions are satisfied there is space in life for actualization of the full possibility of the personality. To achieve at a higher level, much as Socrates suggested. If the basic needs are not fulfilled then much energy is needed to achieve them, particularly in terms of feeding the family and keeping them safe and of having more children to add to the community, then the higher level of purpose may not need to come into play. But in a world with plentiful food in the developed world, with safety being more assured due to highly structured legal mechanisms and law enforcement, sex being a normal part of the modern world, then it might be argued that the self-actualisation, or the need to fulfil some personal potential weighs more heavily on us. Particularly it seems on men, who are much more likely to commit suicide. More so too young men, if they feel shame or a failure, this can become a pressure and they are less likely to ask for help and also more likely to act impulsively.

(Maslow (1943) Psychological Review 50 pp. 370-396. A Theory of Human Motivation Abraham H Maslow, Motivation and Personality, 2nd ed. Chapter 11 "Self-Actualizing People: A Study of Psychological Health")

Whilst Freud worked with mentally ill patients, Maslow decided to work with mentally healthy people, to see what made them so. These were people who had optimal mental health and functioning. He wanted to see why they were so. He found that the healthiest individuals are ones who are in harmony with themselves and their surroundings. He found that the people were very centred and viewed problems rationally which needed solutions. They were happy on their own and had healthy personal relationships with deep friendships and close family rather than shallow relationships.

Maslow remarked that:

'It is as if Freud supplied us the sick half of psychology and we must now fill it out with the healthy half.'

I reflected on this phenomenon when I was in hospital recently with a blood clot in the main artery of my right kidney. I'm still not quite sure, nor are the Doctors, how it came about but suffice to say my right kidney is quite shot and my left kidney is larger than my right and working for two. I had a rather sweet Junior Doctor who was specializing in Nephrology. Of course working in Nephrology you really look at non-functioning or poorly functioning kidneys. He probed around taking the stats with a portable MRI on my right kidney. He was totally thrown by my left kidney. First of all he thought the machine was broken. He did the tried and tested turning it on and off thing. This was not inspiring great confidence in me as I started hyperventilating at the thought that now my left kidney was developing blood clots too. He went for help and the Consultant Nephrologist came to his rescue. They were speaking in German so I wasn't following what was going on at all. Once the Consultant had readjusted the levels of the stats and shown the Junior how to report it he left the room. I then asked in English what on earth was going on? Oh no it's not a problem, I've just not seen a kidney with so much blood going through it before. This young doctor was so used to going around the wards measuring feeble blood flows that he had no idea what a presumably healthy kidney looked like. I thought then how important it is to see healthy and unhealthy people mentally and medically.

Looking at the basic needs paradigm, it would seem logical that if basic needs are not met then there could be a sense of hopelessness. Maybe this is offset in religious countries/populations by strong religious structures that demand you stay alive and keep praying to God. In countries such as Japan and China the God figure does not dictate as a higher power that you should obey. Rather a collective identity is formed with your community that means you would rather sacrifice your life than continue in hopelessness, not providing for your family or not achieving your highest potential. Family and community shame is the ultimate fear.

Conversely in our Western society, in America for example, the individual is the most powerful and important component. You work three jobs to get you through college, you stay up all night to study to improve your grades. It is you, you, you. If you fuck up you are a loser. There is guilt at not being good enough. There are countless examples on social media of beautiful, successful contemporaries who seem to have their shit together. As a therapist I was often amazed after a session with a teenager who was extremely depressed, lonely, failing at school, falling out with their parents, to then have a look at their profile on Facebook. Invariably, as an onlooker you would think they had the most perfect life. Image after image of smiling friends, selfies pouting in the mirror, exotic locations. Life on the web does not reflect real life. In such a competitive environment, where you are not just comparing yourself to the prettiest, funniest, most intelligent or sportiest girl in the class, you can now compare yourself with the rest of the world. It is no wonder that self-esteem can be crippled. But is it enough to kill yourself? In deed girls are more prone to self-harm and develop anorexia or other eating disorders. It is boys who are most likely to kill themselves. So is it their body image, or their sense of maleness, that is so threatened? Or indeed is it something much more biological such as impulse control and lack of as referred to before.

Repeated studies show that boys and young men with poor impulse control are more likely to commit suicide. Poor impulse control is mainly due to brain structure, although there is evidence that impulse control is becoming increasingly poor due to the immediacy of reward via internet, food, tv etc. So there is no boredom. There is no need to wait for anything. If there is a need to wait, then anxiety can mount very easily in test subjects. An American client of mine was bemoaning his son's lack of attention span. He said it's the 8 to 10 minutes theory. I was puzzled? He explained in the US there are adverts every 8 to 10 minutes, so the theory is everyone develops an attention span to reflect that time burst. I had not heard of it because in the UK we have adverts on commercial shows every 15 minutes. But I had not heard of a 15-minute theory in the UK. So there is a dual effect, one our socially and culturally influenced attention span and the other is a biological, neurological difference. I assure you, having worked with children over the years, there are some kids who genuinely cannot pay attention, however much we try and reward their efforts. Within the same family, same upbringing, same environment, same school, a child can suffer with a whole raft of behavioural and academic challenges.

In a world where school, university is all, the pressure on these children, particularly boys is enormous. Self-esteem comes not through doing well at school, but by being the class clown or the bad boy. Next comes drugs, next comes reckless behavior. Some get lucky and calm down a bit in their late 20s. Others don't make it. Certainly the increasing use of party drugs has not helped the suicide rate. MDMA has a reputation for causing dramatic comedowns with some people feeling impossibly depressed for up to a week after taking it. Common references to post MDMA depression is 'Monday blues', 'Suicide Tuesdays' and 'Wasted Wednesdays'. Imperial College London has researched the issue and found ways of avoiding the dramatic comedown that many people experience.

(Research into the effects of MDMA on the resting brain, Channel 4, David Nutt, The Edmond J. Safra Chair in Neuropsychopharmacology and Director of the Neuropsychopharmacology Unit, Imperial College London.)

CHAPTER 20

CORONA VIRUS 19

Whilst writing this book a cultural phenomenon, not known globally since the Spanish flu pandemic at the turn a hundred years ago, has gripped the world in the form of Corona-19. We have more recently seen SARS and MERS and indeed Ebola, but these were for the most part more distant threats that we could assuage our fear by saying, 'ah yes well in Africa they don't really know how to stop transmission…..and the healthcare is not advanced like here…..and it was all started by eating smoked meat that had pathogens' etc. With SARS whilst this did spread more globally, the most affected were the far East, and Hong Kong shocked by the impact both socially and with the pressure on the health system and economically, reacted to COVID-19 decisively. Like Luxembourg, where I am based, Hong Kong is an island. Luxembourg is an island surrounded by countries. Closing the border effectively cuts off half the working staff in hospitals and food supplies not to mention staff in all major services. So the easy containment potential is offset by the suicidal impact on the functioning of the country.

Every country and politician not to mention Joe Bloggs at home has been examining the forecasts, the disease and infection curves, graphs depicting death counts. There is a sort of new religion of scientific and epidemiological gods being rolled out on countless platforms, from major newspapers to local radio stations. I used to work for the Professor of Epidemiology at Cambridge University/Addenbrookes research centre, called amusingly 'Strangeways Laboratory'. Not only did it share its name with a prison, but the various science bods who worked there were as socially awkward as they were brilliant. My boss was probably the most socially at ease which I was why I guess he was the go to person for the BBC to interview, or the Minster for Health to contact for updates on various crises at that time. I found it fascinating.

At the time he was working a lot with controlling of numbers and graphs showing the epidemic effect and impact of BSE (Mad Cow disease). This was the big news story at the time and in much the same way as we had viewed the Chinese outbreaks of the past, with censor and blame for their poor animal welfare and food hygiene causing a catastrophic break down, the UK was under worldwide censure for poor animal husbandry. Cows had been fed with a mixture including sheep's entrails and brains, who had in turn been suffering from Scrapie, a brain disease. This mutated into BSE which caused cows to be infected and then caused the first cases of Human Variant BSE in humans which was a grisly neurological condition which meant a swift death after debilitating neurological shut down of functions. The UK was now the only place in the world where you did not want to eat beef, particularly burgers. Graphs, predictions etc. followed in great number. My professor was heading the UK research into monitoring the crisis and charting its peak. He would explain to me the variables. Previously the disease had not been heard of and therefore no one had been tested for it before, but now increasingly people were being tested for it. Thus the alarming rise in its diagnosis was partly due to it now being tested for. And he showed me a graph of the last five years and you could see a peak and then a level and then a drop. This was after the measures had been taken to stop the use of cattle being fed sheep's remains. There was still the public and human desire to find a safety net. Quite grisly this human need. But I see it again in the Corona virus crisis. Ah so they had underlying health conditions. Oh they were 90. Ah she was only 16 but she was diabetic. This sort of maudlin reassurance at some poor bugger's expense. But we are human. Constantly trying to deny the reality that we move towards a dystopia where normal human emotions are suppressed as being antiquated or primitive. Indeed, they are. Our brains and bodies are driving us just as they always have to survive in communities and in family groups of shared belief systems. We know we are all going to die at some point, but we are trying to avoid it for as long as possible. It is human to feel sad about the death of someone, but equally to be relieved it is not your own child or husband or wife. If we did not have those cares then surely social structures and caring for others would mean we would have a far poorer ability to survive. Structuralism as presented by Levi Strauss. Communities invent Gods and laws to help them survive most effectively.

So my Professor at Strangeways could reassure me that things looked promising as the peak had flattened and we had even noticed a drop last year. But in usual epidemiological expert style, he would end with saying 'but of course it is far too early to be complacent and think that we can be sure that the disease transmission has peaked. We will need to follow the stats for several more years before we can be assured of this as we have no idea presently how long the infection can incubate in the brain (etc.)'. If it sounds familiar to the current crisis, that is because scientists and epidemiologists do not see rates or prediction models in the same way. Even amongst themselves. They are well known for being highly argumentative with each other, it is common practice for a research study to be published only for another expert in another country to pull it apart piece by piece with evidence they have been collating in a study they have been producing. I remember Nick appearing on the BBC in response to a good PR guy Epidemiologist from Sweden who was single handedly doing a good job at undermining the breast cancer scanning programme that Cancer UK and the NHS had painstakingly worked on and publicized in an effort to catch breast abnormalities or stage 1 cancers, so they could be treated early and turn around life expectancy figures for breast cancer survival. This epidemiologist was publishing a very convincing research paper which said that screening was actually more harmful because then women stopped checking their breasts believing that if they had had a clear scan that they were not at risk and need not be self-checking. I can remember Nick was in something of a rage about this guy and caught the train down to London (even in those days he was very sniffy about anyone using a car because of pollution) and appeared on various morning programmes and the news explaining that scanning was vitally important, but that it did not mean that you did not still do a self-check once a week in the bath of your breasts. He was able to show a few bar charts for the average punter to be persuaded that what he said had validity and actually they could see the mortality rates from breast cancer had improved since the regular screening had been made available. Still bristling with scientific indignation he said privately to me, the Swedish epidemiologist was a charlatan and only interested in publicity. The egos in the scientific and medical world are probably more inflated than in other areas of life. They are convinced through science that their idea is right. They have figures to prove it. But as in Psychology you can prove many things with poorly designed studies and the best results come from a compilation of ideas that are not prejudicial against each other. Even the Swedish charlatan maybe helped the British public know that to carry on self-checking was also very important and not just to rely on a yearly scan.

But who would wish to be an epidemiologist or disease control predictor or publish an infection progression model during the current outbreak? It is interesting that the disease, as in SARS, as in BSE has been through transmission of one virus from one species to another. In the current case the wet markets of Wuhan where animals are sold live and so transmission cross species is possible and where hygiene standards are poor, if you are even being generous. And then being eaten by the local population as an exotic delicacy and the jump is then made to humans. The transmission rate with the Covid-19 virus was seen to be extremely high. Despite masks, enforced rules of a lockdown, what appeared to be highly protected health workers in hazmet suits, masks and with face shields, the transmission rate and infection curve escalated into a terrifying picture of people dying in corridors of hospitals. It still seemed far away. Although with the Chinese Government having previously been highly criticized for withholding information regarding the outbreak in November 2002 and reaching its peak in February 2003. From March onwards the disease was detected in other countries, but in Luxembourg patients were not tested for it, despite there being reliable data to suggest that it also reached central Europe. We do not therefore know how many people in reality were affected globally. China wanted to be seen to report on Covid-19 with transparency, but there is no certainty how long they knew about the disease before it was reported to the WHO. And by that time things were in a state of emergency in the city of Wuhan. None of us had probably heard of it before this big event which has had the most severe global ramifications in history. But we now know that the city has 11 million residents, to give it scale London has 9 million. This is a massive urban metropolis which was shut down. There the cultural differences start impacting policy. China is a totalitarian state. People do as they are told. When you role out a model for how to contain this virus and deal with it as a one size fits all model you ignore vital cultural differences. Which is where I bring the focus back to the culture of community versus the culture of the individual and those cultures that lie somewhere in between. China locks down cities with draconian efficiency and with compliance by the affected population. We in the West are not used to obeying authority in the same way.

The UK seems particularly naughty at best, irresponsible at worst. They needed to be given clear rules or they would flout soft advice. This has been my thought process throughout my schooling, throughout my kids schooling and in the work place. People are inventive and if they can find a way around a suggestion they will do so. Soft advice, even hard recommendations are not seen as really applying to them. Now the rules are becoming clearer and clearer. Luxembourg tends to be a bit more Germanic about rules. Despite being essentially a French and a German country and all the other immigrants such as myself living there, it errs more on the Germanic. Socially we tend to follow the rules and there is clear disapproval if they are not followed. I have not witnessed this recently but giving a child a good wallop if they were playing up in a restaurant was not at all frowned upon, but in the UK for quite some years it would be met with some shock. In Scandanavia you would be locked up. In much the same way there is a lot of rules of social thoughtfulness, but rigorously enforced by the commune (the local mayor and council workers). So when we unwittingly mowed the lawn on a Sunday, a Luxembourgish neighbor came round and screamed at us about how it was against the law. As indeed we found out it was. We apologized and stopped. Others have had the commune officials come around and fine them. Everything is rigorously ruled upon. You have to ask the Commune's permission for letting off fireworks and even if you get permission, which would be unlikely, it would be within a specified time frame. Yes, there are quite a few rule breakers on New Year's Eve but generally the rules are abided by. In France they are a rebellious lot. In fact as can be seen in many industrial disputes they are quite happy to enjoy their history of rebellion which is worn as a sort of badge of pride. With countries such as the UK to a lesser extent and in France, where personal liberty is considered a fundamental human right, controlling behavior, even once definitive state of emergency laws have been put in place, is a tough job. Police are becoming heavy handed, some might say petty, going a bit AWOL in pursuing lone walkers in the peaks. There is a sort of social and legal madness because we are unused to having state intervention and being told not to do what we want.

Which brings the subject back to the theme of our control over our own destiny. The nations that look to God put their trust in him. The nations that do not allow a God but the Government is their God to be supported, adored, supplicated to will obey their leader. The individualistic cultures of Europe to a lesser and greater extent take succor in their religion. In the UK fewer people go to church than in any other time in history. As previously discussed this leaves them in a sort of anarchic, individualistic state where only their personal needs are important. If then a life threatening situation presents itself to them, what do they do with that? If anxiety is negated by turning to a higher being, what happens when you have no higher being except yourself. How do you reassure yourself? There has been a succession of social media psychologists, yoga experts, yoga amateurs, anyone with access to an opinion and a platform who are exploding at almost as fast a rate as the virus. Trite soundbites of self-care are everywhere. Helpful tips of gratitude for what you have, making lists of those things you are grateful for. Meditating. Really useful advice like limiting screen time so as not to become obsessed with the terrifying pandemic unfolding would be a first suggestion. Not meditating because actually most of us are at home and do not need to escape a busy world but to do something that feels useful. So physical jobs around the house, baking, reading comedy books or romances, watching upbeat films. Escapism is surely the best way of soothing the soul at this time? How many soldiers would have been any use in the middle of a crisis if they had been sitting in the middle of a battlefield getting in touch with their inner space and smiling at it and being kind to it. I have never heard so much bollocks in my life. Meditation has its place. When fear overwhelms. But that is only useful if you have expended energy to begin with. What people are suffering with at the moment is a lack of expended energy and thus being physically engaged in jobs is surely more beneficial?

The moral dilemma in the Epidemiological response, advice, scientific advisors is do we get through this as quickly as possible and effectively cull the elderly and vulnerable population. Herd immunity. Or do we close down, lock down, stagger transmission rates so we give a chance for hospitals to not be overwhelmed and to shield the elderly until the disease and pestilence has passed. There is a huge sociopolitical question here which involves every aspect of life. It involves the economy, the reserves of the care systems, the sociological and psychological impact of cooped up over 60s, the same concerns over the young isolated at home studying for an uncertain future at home where socioeconomic resources will make a huge impact as to their academic success. There are so many sides to this this dilemma that it seems very unfair to be so mean to the politicians who are attempting to do the right thing without plunging their countries into economic bankruptcy. Sweden as per is the outlier. The socialist, land of equality and good behavior. The sensible pragmatic care to be socially responsible and to just keep a distance. The jury is out as to whether at the final count their approach has been any better than anyone else's, but as I have reiterated throughout this work, no one rule fits all cultures. We have to lean our belief systems towards our cultural histories and our political power dynamics, dependent on whether we live in democracies, monarchies, republics, under communist doctrine or under dictatorships.

Most recently I was rather shocked that the Queen, who normally doesn't put a foot wrong, came under some criticism for being furious that her staff had revolted about leaving their family bubbles to join the staff bubble at Sandringham for Christmas 2020, which means the Queen may have to be forced to spend Christmas at Windsor Castle for the first time in 33 years. I speculated on Facebook that this seemed remarkably tone deaf considering the latest bubble restriction means most of us will not see family at Christmas as per usual. A friend, wittily responded to my post in the comments section saying 'pharaohs required their staff to join them in the pyramid for eternity, so a request for a mere 4 weeks of their private lives sounds rather modest'.

CHAPTER 21

COVID-19 FUNERALS

So as soon as the lockdown became essential in the UK, the Church of England reacted quickly and efficiently to say that funerals would be limited to 5 people, either very close family or friend. The crematoriums were not given this guidance. Crematoriums were bound and still are by government recommendations of 30 mourners. Guidelines are not too helpful when large families or powerful groups are insistent that more be let in to a service. Chapel of rest employees, a vicar or a celebrant are not security guards, and so attempt to accommodate the needs of the grievers, at risk to their own health.

Indeed my mother-in-law died during the covid pandemic. She had advanced dementia and normally would have been admitted to hospital, but died a seemingly peaceful death in her nursing home with one of her sons and daughter with her. She was able to say goodbye to the rest of the family via facetime calls. Modern technology helping give some comfort to her and to her family. The funeral was attended with social distancing and the funeral home ushered in and out family members discreetly, so that whilst there were no more than permitted in the funeral at the same time, they could take it in turns to be a part of the service. We watched via zoom, organized by the funeral home.

What was missing, apart from physically being there, was the wake, the after get together where stories could be shared and her life celebrated. There was a zoom get together. But it's not quite the same.

I was discussing this with my local Anglican vicar who said that the Church of England could use precedent for their decision to delay funerals. Canada has always needed to delay funerals from an entirely practical point of view that the ground is frozen for the best part of winter and graves cannot be dug. So if a cremation is wanted then all well and good, but for those who wished to be buried in hallowed grounds, their relatives must wait until spring before the funeral can take place. In many ways this must be like the popular practice now of having a small funeral shortly after death followed by a Memorial Service where a wider circle of relatives, friends, colleagues can attend and there is a lighter more celebratory nature of the ceremony. Whether this will satiate the need to grieve in the same way emotionally it is hard to say, this being unprecedented in most countries. In Canada emotionally they are already prepared culturally for this, but we are not. This is a new territory and we have no cultural history to base it on. We are not emotionally prepared to do things in this way.

Three weeks into this the UK lockdown during this pandemic of covid-19, I am reading an article in 'The Sun' newspaper. For the well-educated, The Sun is the everyday paper for the common man/woman. Once famous for its page 3 photo of a topless model, ironically the most loved Linda Lusardi during the 80s, has recently overcome a very serious fight for life after contracting covid-19. Not within the vulnerable age bracket and with no prior health vulnerabilities, she was shell shocked by this virus. But the articles I believe are the most interesting because they tell the mass public what they might not know and are interested in knowing. Today 14/04/2020 there is an article by Daniel Hammond talking about mass graves being dug in South East London as the number of dead continues to mount. 'The Plots, which are ten yards long and two yards wide, were created at Kemnal Park Cemetery in Chiselhurst for the members of the Islamic community. At the moment they have 50 people waiting for burial as an Islamic burial should take place within 24 hours of death. The so-called 'saff graves' (Arabic for rows) are said to be in accordance with the Muslim faith. Head of the cemetery Richard Gomersall said *'Funerals will take place in quick succession and in accordance with Islamic practice. We will not be cutting any corners'*. A vast temporary mortuary is in Wanstead Flats, East London. Another temporary mortuary has been constructed at the 10 acre Low Hall Depot site in Waltham Forest.

Soldiers have meanwhile been drafted in as security at London's Nightingale hospital. The military have been helping with planning and building at facility at the ExCel Centre and planning four new hospitals. Troops have delivered protective equipment while others will become ambulance drivers.

So as the military becomes an integral part of this 'fight' as the politicians and press have constantly portrayed this as, the involvement of the military certainly adds to the imagery. It is reminiscent of the earlier chapter discussing our use of battle imagery against cancer. It is emotive language to give us some energy and feeling of agency, preventing us from feeling like victims. All the hand washing and disinfecting, distancing, storing of food, creating of social network groups with activities, is all part of a 'blitz' mentality. And so is the language of the leaders of separate nations. Trying to prop up the morale of the nation, clapping health workers at the same time every evening as a way of keeping our spirits up and honoring our protectors. America is good at this. Their social system is geared at respect. They salute the flag. They are for the most part Christians who feel no embarrassment in proclaiming their faith in God or indeed the fact that God blesses America. As a self-critical nation (perhaps born out of post-imperialist guilt), the UK is poor at praising itself. The press normally put down everything about us. Our ability to run a decent economy, have good food, be lawful, have community spirit, but the biggest hang up is how to hold on to our NHS. Like a frail old lady that we love and must protect. It is staggering how obsessed the collective mentality of the Brits and the precious NHS rules politics. It is almost heretical to suggest healthcare is organized in a different way financially.

Mass hysteria breaks out. And immediately parallels are drawn with America where poor are left dying on the street in the hope a community hospital might pick them up. To draw a parallel with the German Health Service, which has been a shining example of an efficient health service which has kept deaths lower than other European countries of similar size, could be useful. But of course like any other death, it is not only the death that is down to the ICU. It is socially relevant, level of elderly in the country, social housing and proximity of peoples, social norms of mixing, greeting etc. It is multi-faceted. You only have to hang around Italians for a while and know they are more tactile, speak closer to you than a Brit is comfortable with, kiss more, hug more, hold hands etc. I used to work in an Italian bank and was astonished to see the middle aged bankers walk off to lunch, frequently holding hands or arm in arm, like we used to do as school children. These are different cultures and as such disease can be spread differently. The French kiss a lot. Just as a normal greeting. In the supermarkets at the start of a shift and end of a shift an employee will go down the entire length of the cashier tills giving the 3 kiss hello or goodbye. As a customer you just wait and then the cashier carries on scanning. Absolutely normal for them. The French press has repeated begged their nationals to stop kissing. It's a hard habit for them to break.

Listening to a Swedish Epidemiologist today on a web platform, he was answering questions as to Sweden's extraordinary decision to make suggestions re some social distancing, whilst still allowing primary schools to function, gatherings of up to 50 people to take place, but limiting access to Old People's Homes. The Epidemiologist said that in fact that the deaths in Sweden were comparable to other countries that had full lockdowns and so to continue with lockdown is not an evidence based decision. The interviewer pointed out that deaths amongst the elderly in Sweden was much higher than in Norway. His response, again alludes to social organization, that in Norway Old People's Home are quite small and so an infection once in could be contained better or there would be a natural limit to how many of the elderly would succumb to the disease. In Sweden however, Old People's Homes are very large and so if an infection occurs in one then the mortality will be much higher.

In Detroit Medical Center Sinai-Grace nurses leaked to the press that bodies were accumulating in hospital storage rooms. New York hospitals and funeral homes arranged refrigerated trucks to store bodies. More than 600 bodies were reported to be frozen in trucks on the Brooklyn waterfront because next of kin can either not be located, they also are sick or they cannot afford to pay for a burial.

In Montana it was reported that the hospital was running at capacity and that they are letting relatives say goodbye through windows, holding up computer tablets with their last words.   In a poor area of Texas county officials are using covid-19 funds to help cover the burial costs for impoverished families. They were concerned that families were losing multiple members of their family in the space of weeks. The traditional ritual of support from funeral homes and the church no longer available due to the vast numbers of dead, they decided to ask anyone to send out a photo of a loved one who had died of covid-19.   Carlos Sanchez the county spokesperson, who himself had survived the virus, said that *'Within minutes, we got more than 20 emails. Several sent photos of multiple relatives. They want them to be remembered'*

So we have our battle imagery.   We are going into battle against a virus, an invisible enemy.   Some scientists have hoped to spread the message with virtual modelling of how a cough can pass thousands of droplets of the virus through air currents and systems, for example in a supermarket.   Over food, onto the floor, over aisles.   And yet there is our social norm which powerfully supercedes this imaging. If you make too big of an issue about avoiding someone in an aisle you don't want to look rude. Equally now the other side of our 'war' analogy takes shape.   We don't want people to infect us. We are not living in times of the plague, although we are, we are not painting a red cross on our door to say we have the plague or ringing a bell. We are allowing people to know through social media, phone calls etc. In fact, such is the social media explosion that we know about everyone and their cat, literally with regards a couple of cats who have got the virus in China. Admittedly we are told they caught the virus off their owners, so people mustn't panic and start abandoning their pets as we cannot catch covid-19 from our dogs and cats. Although their fur could hold the virus and if we stroked them we could, if they had been in contact with another dog whose owner had got covid and some of the viral shed had landed on their fur etc. So we read and read this information. Most of us without the scientific knowledge do not know how to make sense of it, but the fear is ratcheted up. So the pooch gets a disinfectant wash and is not allowed to play with other dogs.

Other factors, that I had foreseen, was the misinformation given out about masks. There was an early panic that the highest risk workers, nurses, cleaners, social carers, social workers, hospital administrators, GPs, GP receptionists, pharmacists etc., would not get enough PPE to stay safe from viral infection. In deed such was the panic that, in my view, a plethora of misinformation was spread about how wearing a mask could be more likely to give you the virus as you could put it right next to your nose or mouth as you put it on or took it off. It was not just that the common read every day was they didn't work but that also running right next to that was the desperate cry for supplies of masks for 'key workers', the bi-word of this pandemic. So how logical is that? On the one hand they are trying to persuade us they don't work and on the other hand they are raging that so many key staff do not have them? It was clear that the idea was to stop most of us stock piling masks for our own benefit so that key workers could have them. But to give misinformation is cynical. Even to the point where if you wore masks people would try and humiliate you and say, they don't work you know. Or you have the wrong sort. Now we are three weeks in to the lockdown in the UK and slightly longer in Luxembourg. And now of course they are encouraging people to wear masks, if they have them, or if they can make homemade ones which can be washed at high temperature.

Elsewhere in the UK the police have taken over control in a slightly dystopic fashion. Riding into parks telling sunbathers to go home. Neighbours being encouraged to grass up their neighbours for having friends over etc. It is our version of being given the white feather during the WW1 for cowardice. People are watching each other and making sure they are not breaking the laws. When you are trying to exist in a life and death situation you feel enabled to behave in a way that you might not ordinarily. I had a personal experience of this in the supermarket in Luxembourg. There were big signs up telling us to go in alone, keep distance and if we picked something up to buy it. Fairly obvious advice. Well a rule. And a woman was working her way through every avocado in a box squeezing it and then for some reason sniffing it. So I had one of those waves of rage and said, in English, 'why don't you touch and sniff all of them, make sure you don't miss any out?' This is our famous British sarcasm at play. I do anyway take such articles home and spray them with bleach, then wipe over with hot water. But whilst you can do that with an avocado, you can't for an apple. It enraged me. I do not want to die because some stupid woman wanted to choose the most perfectly ripe avocado during a pandemic. This typifies the war we are having. It is not being rooted out by Nazi's. It is a middle class war. An indulgent war. Everyone wanting to have the loveliest time and food whilst in isolation. It is the Nigella Lawson of wars.

Much of this book has been emphasizing that death is a physical event but with a diverse cultural response and historical response to it. What comforts families in death is their cultural norm for dealing with it. The comfort is in the tradition. In uncertainty and emotional upheaval, sorting out effects, organizing the list of who should know, preparing a newspaper entry of death, organizing the funeral and the service. Picking out hymns and pieces of music are all, as a Psychologist would see as 'distracting activities' that help focus on practicalities and delay the shock of the loss. By the time the funeral is done some time has passed. The attention falls away. Letters of condolence can be put away and grieving can begin in earnest. There is a pattern to grief that culturally we are aware of. Not that people deal with it in the same way. Grief is personal. But there do seem to be some common stages of grief. Not necessarily in a definitive order. But emotions tend to form a similar focus and change as the individual processes their grief. Much as in our modern world we would love a quick fix, there does not seem to be one. Indeed 'rushing to recovery' normally is a faulty mechanism which means that the griever will suddenly nosedive into depression at a later point. Equally some people are more resilient and pragmatic about death and do not feel as emotionally poleaxed as others. Which leads to the next area to be considered, which is grief.

CHAPTER 22

GRIEF

From a Psychotherapist's perspective, we normally enter into a person's grief story when the grief has become untenable for either them or their family. Looking at grieving in communities, as has been outlined, there are social customs, rituals, expected reactions, varied responses depending on the personality involved and their relationship with the deceased. The events that led to the death of an individual, expected, sudden, motor accident, cancer, suicide. There are so many different variables and as a Psychotherapist, the central issue is always the feelings are the client's. They belong only to them. In other words that grief is essentially entirely personal and varied. But we call a 'complicated grief', that which causes problems to the individual in moving on. The following indicate signs of a complicated grief:

Case Study on the persistence of denial with delayed or no grieving

An extraordinarily bright young girl was faced with the sudden loss of her mother just before her A levels. Claudine was super bright. Always top grades. She wanted to study medicine. Her exams were due in June and in March of that year her mother suddenly was diagnosed with stage 4 Ovarian cancer. She lasted

6 weeks. So from no knowledge of anyone in the family that the mother was ill, to her dying very quickly and leaving behind a grieving husband, Anna and her younger brother and sister. Only Claudine was not distraught. At the funeral friends of her mothers were weeping and attempting to say the right thing to Claudine. They were trying to hug her, engage, saying dire cliché's like 'I'm sorry for your loss'. Claudine commented years later that the best thing that anyone said to her at the funeral was her Mum's best friend who said simply 'This is shit isn't it?'. A kind of raw honesty that meant something to Claudine.

Claudine didn't cry, carried on studying very hard for her exams. Aced the lot of them. Went on all the girl trips to sunny locations after the exams and before she started med school. Her med studies continued brilliantly, she became a Doctor and then after two years of working in a hospital she thought, 'I don't have to cure cancer' and 'I'm not sure I can handle seeing patients die'. She found it wasn't gratifying personally. She also accepted that the grief goes into your DNA and never leaves. And so she left her job as a Doctor, her childhood dream, and now runs a marketing team. She loves the team, gets paid well, of course keeps getting promotions, but most importantly she doesn't have to deal with heavy emotions every day. Plus, she can have lots of time with her boyfriend who she lives with.

So Claudine had a complicated grief. Some women thought it odd how cold and detached she looked at the funeral. Typically, Claudine, who had argued a lot with her Mum and was rather closer to her father, shrugged off theoretical ideas of complicated grief due to conflicted self or guilt. Claudine just saw that she was feeling a certain way inside and did not need to prove anything to anyone with a reaction.

Possibly with the above example, an intervention with therapy at an early stage might have mitigated the longer extent of the grief and the fact that she now sees it as part of her DNA that will never go away. We might say that she is stuck in grief. But to go to therapy on the whole is a voluntary action. Dragging resistant teens to therapy, I can attest to, is a highly counterproductive strategy by their parents. And to all extents and purposes Claudine was not getting wildly drunk or being wildly irresponsible. She just wanted to get on with it. And that can be true of many teenagers. Because they do not like being outside of the norm, or to get attention that singles them out. This is a generalization, but I have heard many times in therapy that a teenager does not want their parent's death to define them. The kid whose Mum died in 6th grade. This gives them a sort of social cache that no one would want. Being 'pitied' or 'patronized' or 'mummied' by well-meaning friends. They don't want a new Mummy. They had their Mum and they accept that now they don't.

Progressive Social Isolation

Another sign of reactive depression, typical of grief, is a retreat into isolation. Not going to school or work. Finding engaging with others too exhausting or pointless. This retreat from the world is perceived culturally as normal in the first instance of grief. But if the perceived time scale is overrun and the person is still not back functioning socially then it is deemed a 'problem grief'. I remember a guy I used to work with years ago. He was something of a nerd and had been married for 20 years to his lovely wife. They were a couple who had decided not to have children, because their life was so great as it was that they did not feel the need to add to it. They used to go on cruises and both were keen walkers. His wife died. On that day so did he as such. Or his whole life as he knew it. I think the bank that I was working in called him up after two weeks and said, more or less, look it has been two weeks. I can remember, aged 25, thinking how bloody heartless it was. This guy not only had lost his wife but now was having pressure on him to get back to work, as two weeks was not enough time in their view for him to get his shit together and start working again. He came back, a shadow of his former self. Nothing to talk about. But in a funny way the bank forced him to get out of his social isolation. It's sometimes helpful to have reality kick you out of the front door however obscene it looks at the time. With people who do not have jobs to go to their social isolation can become increasingly problematic. A child may start refusing to go to school if a parent has died. The remaining parent is therefore conflicted by their own grief and what they should do.

Case Study

Philippa lost her Mum unexpectedly and suddenly one weekend. Her Mum had gone to Cambridge shopping and come home feeling a bit peaky. She said she felt rough and could someone bring her up a cup of coffee as she couldn't face supper. The cup of coffee was duly served to her and later that evening her husband came to bed and she was sleeping. In the morning he found her dead. She had had a heart attack during the night. She had no knowledge of an issue with her heart. The father was grieving, the older sister away now at University was grieving, the younger sister was stuck in grief and was suffering when I saw her with hypochondria. Not surprisingly she had panicked that she might have some inherited heart default and had had a vast array of tests over the previous year in an attempt to reassure her. With school refusal, loss of all her friends (who were now irritated by her), no physical reassurance working it was time for therapy. And during therapy she grieved for the what if's. The what if her Mum hadn't gone to Cambridge shopping?. What if she'd gone with her? What if she had gone up after the cup of coffee and checked her and called a Doctor? There were so many what if's? We dealt with all of them with clinical precision. It all came down to one thing and that was she felt impotent as to what had happened and now she felt isolated and so her thoughts turned obsessively to her body and how fast her heart was beating. I find it helps in hypochondriac patients to deal with the ultimate and then, and then, and then in scenarios. To really put it to them. So you don't rescue yourself, you don't stay out of danger, you don't do anything and you collapse at school. What would happen? Yes they would call an ambulance. And if you had been at home alone it would be worse right hypothetically? Because you would be on your own.

It ended up with Philippa that she was having multiple panic attacks and by retreating each time it was reinforcing the problem. So we worked on panic attacks and how to see them through and why they happen, and what happens clinically to your blood and breathing during a panic attack etc. Philippa was a bright girl. She got it. She then panicked about her school work and she lost an entire dissertation by not saving the document. We agreed there was a certain amount of self-sabotage. But it helped because then we could say, what do you think your Mum would suggest. She laughed and said her Mum would say she was being a plonker. It was one of those lightbulb moments where you just saw how much she missed her humorous, no nonsense Mum.

Anger

A very Common reaction to grief is Anger. When it becomes paranoid and litigious towards the medical staff that were caring for their loved ones at the end it can be time consuming for the health service to deal with. It is as if the person needs someone to blame, however irrational. There is this huge emotional feeling that needs to blast in a direction. Any direction. And clearly the nursing home, hospital, Doctor who didn't spot it fast enough etc., is blamed and is on the receiving end of the anger. Such is the frequency of these events that there are stages of procedure to deal with helping the complainer make sense of what happened and why things happened in the order they did. But again getting stuck in grief can mean that years after the event, a person can still be rolling out the resentment as to how their loved one died.

Case Study

Hilary lost her mother to a pulmonary embolism when she was 35. Her mother had had breast cancer and had succeeded in 'beating' it as Hilary would describe it. But a few weeks after the all clear was given her mother suddenly was rushed back into hospital with a pulmonary embolism. Hilary did not even have time to say her goodbyes in the hospital. Some years later Hilary commented that due to her Mum being an alcoholic, the Doctors said that the pulmonary embolism was just one way her Mum was going to die that year. Her liver was like a doily, such was the

damage that a lifetimes drinking had had on it. Her mother always had weeks to live. It was fascinating that Hilary always focused on the' bloody hospital' that had not saved her from dying with the pulmonary embolism. This example is one of projection. Projecting away from any accountability as regards her Mum to her drinking and blaming the authorities for not saving her Mum. You project the problem to a third party to keep your loved one sacrosanct.

The above example is maybe again an example of how in the absence of a God to revere and accept his decision, we need to blame another God and in today's secular society Doctors are the new gods. The ones who know everything and can tell us how our mortality is looking. In days gone past and in other cultures where religion is still a leading force then an angry, grief stricken individual might rage at the heavens and God. Now lawsuits are taken out against hospitals and care homes. Humans have innate behavioral patterns and when the social framework is muddy they have to turn that behavior somewhere or on to someone.

Hyperactivity/Avoiding Grief

Another 'faulty' grieving pattern is hyperactivity without grieving. So the client is avoiding stopping because their greatest fear is if they stop then the grief is going to hit them with an insurmountable force. So they are going to not let that happen. To do this they are going to be busy, busy, busy. Project after project, marathon runs, obsessively working, signing up to everything in sight. Everyone around them watches with apprehension waiting for the inevitable crash. Some clients come to me several years after a loss. They may have thrown themselves at everything and the kitchen sink to avoid grieving and they feel ridiculous turning up at therapy saying, I want grief therapy, my Dad died 8 years ago. There is a pattern of a person having diverted their attention so successfully into child rearing for example, or in pursuing their career, that any human need for grief has not been catered for. Then something happens, the catalyst. It could be they lose their job. It could be the kids leave home for University and suddenly in their new grief, the old grief that was not catered for at the time, rears its head. So something generally comes as a catalyst and when this happens it as if the person is just knocked off their feet. So the very thing that they were trying so assiduously to avoid for all those years happens and they are left winded and blindsided. But because it happened so many years ago, none of their friends get it, their family don't get it. In fact, they themselves don't get it. Why now? And so the therapy is working through the memories of the person they lost. What their relationship was like? What did they argue about? What did they laugh about? What did they have in common?

The therapy is exactly the same 8 or 10 years after the event as it might be 6 months after the event. Photos can be shown. That can help keep the conversation flowing. Because this person feels a fool talking to anyone else about it, the therapist is their guilty time, if you like, when they can indulge in memories. And the therapist gives them permission to grieve. Part of the responsibility still though is that the person does not get stuck in grief. So the resolution of the therapy with grief counselling is highly sensitive. Because it is another end. And in this case, it is the end of the space and time when you could talk about the person you are grieving for. For that reason, there has to be scaffolding for the client to know is in place for their self-care afterwards. That is worked through with the client. Repeating how they can make their time for grief. Repeating how the client is going to work out when they are feeling bad and what their strategy will be. So the social isolationist will need a strategy of forced interaction on several days a week and work up to more. The hyper distractor client will need to say, hang on I'm being a bit too busy at the moment, maybe I need to diarize some nothing time. Just sit in the garden and write some thoughts. Go for a walk and let my mind meander about the past and how I feel about things. It's so much easier with religion. You go to a church and light a candle when you feel the grief. You kiss some religious artefacts to bring you blessings and to bring blessings to your loved ones in heaven. Working out strategies of self-care with your therapist is very cold and calculating. There is no elevation of spirit. It is clinical.

Covid19 grieving has added another phenomenon to the grieving process. Two widows I know have spoken movingly about the space that isolation left for grieving. One widow lost her husband three years ago, but with an early commute to the city to work out in the gym at her workplace, then as head of PR she was busy all day, then maybe a quick drink with a friend after work and then home to her 'sanctuary' as she called the house that she and her husband had built on the banks of the Moselle river. She enjoyed her evenings quietly, looking out at the view. It was during lockdown that the grief swept in. She described that had he been still alive, her husband would have made lockdown fun. Just the two of them. John always bought the party she said, eyes misting up. We would have had the best time just us two. Yeah she added, I really felt the hole he has left in my life. It wasn't so obvious when I was going in to the office every day, but being on your own all day and all evening.

Another widow said that the lockdown had also been extremely isolating for her. She admits that even though it is seven years since her husband died, every morning she wakes up and thinks, oh no he's gone. Which sounds so incredibly sad and yet incredibly lovely in the sense that they must have had such a wonderful marriage. I hear his voice in my youngest son, she said.

When I hear him laugh in another room it could be my husband. So whilst she would normally meet with friends and play golf, see her sons and their families and generally live an active and full life, this lockdown had her isolated and the hole that her husband has left in her life stared at her like a chasm.

It's an irony as another divorcee remarked, that many in miserable marriages might be ironically relieved if their spouse died. Although these are usually complicated griefs. The guilt of failure in a relationship is much harder to grieve than a pure love for someone. However painful the grief is, it is more straightforward. Sadness and longing. Hopefully in time smiling at memories.

Collective Grief

Collective grief is the time honored tradition of grieving in a culturally appropriate manner. As much of this work has testified, normal grieving patterns are increasingly threatened with the ego culture. No longer a standard practice of mourning attire, black, or wearing black for a certain period of time as a widow to show respect and dignify the loss. Songs are chosen, themes are adapted, attempts are made to be happy about it all, desperately fighting the human need to be miserable and cry. The wailing hysterics of North Korea showing collective grief over a lost leader, possibly for fear of being killed if they do not, maybe a cathartic experience we can once more learn from. If William and Harry had been allowed to weep and wail when their mother died, like the rest of the nation did, maybe they would both not be so stuck in their grief today. The trauma of having to walk behind her coffin with a stiff upper lip is perhaps the most dehumanizing sight we have witnessed. That is not to say that a formal event to respect the loss of someone is not very much needed and appropriate, but let them cry. Encourage them to cry and have someone comfort them.

Prince William and Prince Harry have spent a lot of time and effort concentrating on the need to address mental health, particularly men. They have made speeches and supported mental health platforms that encourage men to not feel too proud not to exhibit and experience feelings. Prince William said recently that men need to be encouraged to open up and talk about their feelings. Of course this approach flies in the face of the normal edit of the Royal Family to put up and shut up. To experience all emotions behind closed doors and not to expose weakness to their subjects. This has traditionally been seen as a duty by the Queen, although Queen Victoria certainly took grieving to a new level with her black widower's dress for years after Bertie had died.

Prince William and Prince Harry were not really accommodated for in their grief. They were hastily assigned a mother substitute and had their time ram packed with activity, so much so that the grief that was stuck within them would take years to emerge when finally there was a space for it to be accessed. So they use their experience, not of losing the most iconic woman of the 20th century, but simply of losing their Mum as a way of relating to those in suffering who they meet in their service. Now Prince Harry has left the firm and can maybe allow himself to express his emotions as he sees fit and not to conform to the narrative that he and William had assumed together as brothers. Maybe as he grows in his relationship with Meghan and with his new role as a father, with a wife he loves, he can find new ways to grieve and even celebrate the life of his mother. It is a challenge because of the missing years where maybe his grief could have been expressed in a healthier way, but he is certainly still young enough to find a way forward with his grief. William meanwhile, from what sources report, has found a very close bond with his parents-in-law. A happily married couple who have lived in their community for years and are much protected by it despite their public profile. He has developed a close relationship with Catherine's parents and this relationship possibly resembles the kind of close loving and unstuffy one that Princess Diana attempted to provide for her boys. With plenty of physical contact and cuddles and love. When they were in a room Diana only had eyes for them and vice versa. This in such a cold, austere environment as the palace has been depicted with courtiers in charge of behavior and decorum, seems to have been an impossible place to process emotions.

CHAPTER 23

SO WHAT THEN OF THE FUTURE?

The book has covered many topics associated with death and grieving, with structural systems that protect our communities, with rituals that give space for emotions to be processed and with ever changing rituals emerging through social media and the constant communication channel that it provides to most of us. We hear about more deaths but are shielded from seeing them. We have heard about the huge amount of deaths per week during covid globally but, unless you are working in a hospital, a morgue or a funeral home one might not know a thing about it. How will this pan out emotionally for people?

The first images of Wuhan showed grainy pictures of people collapsing in the streets, in hospital corridors, bodies being piled up in rooms. We sanitize the images, but they are there still. In mass temporary morgues all over America and in the United Kingdom, covid victims are stored in conditions reminiscent of war time. We remain hidden for the most parts from these realities. But the people who are dealing with these deaths on a daily basis are really suffering. The sheer scale of deaths, the stress on the health workers to provide high skilled medical care whilst offering palliative care at the same time is unprecedented. In earlier times the responsibilities for all these cares would have been at home. The nursing, praying and comforting. All these actions were home based not structurally taken over by institutions, by hospitals and medical protocol. The doors daubed with a cross to indicate the plague would allow neighbours to stay clear. Now we stay within our homes but no one really knows who has the virus and who does not. Only via social media and statistics. It is a different kind of dying. A modern dying, but one that creates a huge pressure on health professionals to fulfil multiple roles.

Death is the most normal thing in life. But most of us do not see it. It lies camouflaged in ceremony and discreet movements that hide the face of it from us, unless we have been directly involved. It remains to be seen whether this is human? Whether we can process death if we are denied it's sight whilst others are left to deal with it in such vast numbers?

Printed in Great Britain
by Amazon

56371768R00132